JOHN GIBSON won the first ever British Sports Journalism Award in 1982 and has become a regular winner of both the National and North East Regional awards ever since. In all he has topped 20 awards including the prestigious Wilkinson Sword from Sport Newcastle for services to sport in the city.

He began his career on the Hexham Courant weekly newspaper and spent four years in Fleet Street with The Sun but made his name and reputation with the Evening Chronicle in Newcastle covering Newcastle United before becoming executive sports editor.

Gibson has regularly reported on World Cup finals since England's memorable victory of 1966 as well as the Olympic Games across the globe.

In a diverse career he also owned a football club (Gateshead in the Conference), made TV documentaries, took chat shows round the North East, and is an author with a prodigious output. This is his 17th book.

However he still doesn't know what he wants to do when he grows up!

D1420130

To my lovely daughters Sally, Deborah and Claire and my equally lovely grandson Max.

Thanks for all the joyous memories.

John Gibson

The
GIBBO
FILES

Sport Media ⬥

Foreword

THE Gibbo Files? **Where do I begin? John Gibson, legendary writer, larger than life iconic Geordie! Massive Toon Fan, Grandfather, Father, Best friend, Hero!**

If you were a 12-year-old boxer from the ass end of the North-East, getting the legendary John Gibson to write your name in the Chronicle was like winning an Oscar, touching the FA Cup, getting a kiss off Marilyn Monroe. It's like been made by the Mafia. You've arrived.

I became a Made man at 16 when I lifted the national amateur boxing title in London. He was there, he has been there every day since; seen me fight at every level, winning British and Commonwealth titles and becoming the first North-East World Champion ever.

He has phoned me every week of my life, I have phoned him every week of my life. He was with me every step of the way through my boxing career from Vegas to Moscow. He laughed and cried with me in my career from Mike Tyson to Lennox Lewis.

We have travelled the globe together from Stanley to Shanghai. We have met the biggest stars, the greatest sportsmen and Hollywood legends. We locked Sugar Ray out of the gym and we ran away from a gun-toting Olympic legend!

John is and has been my best friend my whole adult life, but he is more than that. I've looked up to him for as long as I can remember. I love literature. I learnt to read because of my passion for boxing; Hemingway, Hausser, Hart, and John Gibson our very own literary legend.

"Goodness Gracious Great Balls of Fire," – no, it wasn't written about Gibbo (I think!) but Jerry Lee did sing it to him aptly enough when we brought him to City Hall, Newcastle, for his remembrance concert.

We have produced documentaries, promoted concerts, organised celebrity parties. We have had tea with gangland villains in L.A., enjoyed monumental nights in the Ghettos of Mexico, and danced on the beaches of Cuba!

I've been lucky enough to spend the best part of four decades with my friend, my colleague and my hero. We have travelled the world, ate and drank at the poorest and richest of tables, and sure enough we've raised some hell and have touched heaven.

It's been one amazing ride. Bonnie had Clyde, Butch had Sundance, I'm blessed that Glenn had Gibbo!

I'm sure you will find this story, this life, as incredible as I have found it. And will continue to find it.

GLENN McCRORY
Former British, Commonwealth and World
cruiserweight champion & Sky TV commentator

The
GIBBO
FILES

Sport Media 🌑

By John Gibson

Published by Trinity Mirror Sport Media
Managing Director: Ken Rogers
Publishing Director: Steve Hanrahan
Senior Editor: Paul Dove
Executive Art Editor: Rick Cooke
Design and Production: Michael McGuinness and Simon Monk
Cover Design: Colin Harrison
Senior Marketing Executive: Claire Brown

Paperback Edition.
Published in Great Britain in 2014.
Published and produced by: Trinity Mirror Sport Media,
PO Box 48, Old Hall Street, Liverpool L69 3EB

Copyright: John Gibson

All Rights Reserved. No part of this publication may be reproduced, stored
in a retrieval system, or transmitted in any form, or by any means, electronic,
mechanical, photocopying, recording or otherwise without the prior
permission in writing of the copyright holders, nor be otherwise circulated in
any form of binding or cover other than in which it is published and without
a similar condition being imposed on the subsequent publisher.

ISBN: 9781908695987

Photographic acknowledgements:
John Gibson personal collection,
Trinity Mirror (Daily Mirror, Newcastle Journal &
Evening Chronicle), PA Photos

Printed and bound by CPI Group (UK) Ltd, Croydon, CR0 4YY

Contents

A job for life

I FIRST saw the half light of a grim day shortly after Adolf Hitler plunged the world into darkness for six years. My birthday was January 4, 1941. Easy to remember: 4-1-41.

As a consequence of a brutally destructive war my early memories are of my Donald Duck gas mask, sirens and air raid shelters visited at ungodly hours, and a barrage balloon knocking the top off the spire of our local church. Instead of playing games in the back yard I lovingly retrieved a piece of shrapnel which had fallen next to the ashbin and placed it on cotton wool inside a matchbox. Ah, the spoils of war.

With my dad fighting Rommel in the desert, mam moved to live with her mam in a house above Thompson's Red Stamp Store on Benwell's Adelaide Terrace in the west of the city. I never left as a kid. German prisoners of war were digging the roads, trolley buses trundled past our front door, the top deck engulfed by black smoke from countless Woodbines, and one suspected conscientious objector who walked the streets devoid of young men off fighting was regularly spat upon.

The rag and bone man trundled up our back lane once a week, the illegal bookie operated out of a back yard just round the corner, and the fish man selling out of the back of his van once turned his cleaver the wrong way round to chop an over eager cat getting too close. The blood splattered my boots.

We had no hot water and the electricity was governed by a meter. What there was. There was none in the kitchen. It was an outside netty which meant a top coat over your pyjamas if you were to venture forth on winter nights. A tin bath in front of the fire was a weekly ritual and a mangle up in the attic was essential on wash day. The walls were badly enough pointed for me to have to rub the green mould off the inside before venturing to bed. When I wasn't collecting shrapnel I was amusing myself by sprinkling salt on the tails of the snails which dared venture onto our kitchen bench at the first sign of darkness.

Yet I was happy enough. I didn't feel badly done to at all. Why should I? Everyone else I knew lived exactly the same way as us. The rich folk never bothered venturing into Benwell. What we did have was a tremendous sense of community spirit. Perhaps it had something to do with the war but we didn't fear those around us and never bothered about bolting the back door. We weren't going to be robbed. What were they going to pinch?

Whereas all the kids round the doors wanted to play football for Newcastle United I wanted to write about those who did. Funny isn't it? I never dreamed of wearing the famed black and white stripes but I meticulously cut out pictures of Wor Jackie, Joe Harvey, Frank Brennan and Bobby Mitchell from the papers, stuck them in a scrapbook my grandmother made by folding brown paper in half and sewing along the spine, and proceeded to write words of wisdom underneath.

FA Cup final day was extra special. My grandmother, who I came to call mother (as opposed to mam) because I lived with her for the rest of my childhood years, used to make me a massive rosette in the colours of whichever team I wanted to support. She did it with the remnants of the clippy mat she was busy working on.

There I was, a rosette as big as me, sitting in front of our radio listening to words of sheer poetry from Wembley. By the time Newcastle made the three FA Cup finals of the early fifties my Aunt Grace had acquired the only telly in the family, a black and white one the size of a postage stamp, and we all went to her house to sit in long rows of wooden chairs watching Wor Jackie et al become habitual winners. Honestly, I thought it was going to be like this for the rest of my life. Was I in for a rude awakening!

My first job in newspapers was at the *Hexham Courant*. I used to walk down the steep cobbles past the terraced houses of Scotswood and get on the train to the beautiful little market town strolling up to the office opposite the Abbey. It was, still is, a weekly paper which meant I had several days to polish my match reports after watching Hexham Hearts, Stamfordham or whoever played on the Saturday. Time I needed.

I covered everything for the *Courant* from courts to funerals, council meetings to gatherings of Jehovah's Witnesses, marts to flower shows. However I knew where my future lay and I wouldn't join the *Evening Chronicle* who came calling until I was guaranteed a job on sport.

I graduated to Fleet Street simply because at that time I believed it was the place every decent hack should aspire to be at some stage of his career. Doctors aimed for Harley Street, we for the hostelries of Fleet Street.

Sure, sport has opened many doors for me. I've met men of genius, those who thought they had genius, colourful characters and crazy nuts. It's been a privilege because all brought something to the table. However legends aren't confined to those who perform. Those who write can become great raconteurs, infamous drinkers and never to be forgotten men of letters. I met many in Fleet Street and since.

Like the great Geoffrey Green of *The Times*, a delightful man whose personal catchphrase was "every day is Christmas Day." Born in India, he won a soccer Blue at Cambridge University and played for Corinthian Casuals. Once he persuaded Louis Armstrong, sustained by several whiskeys, to climb into his college at Cambridge and spend a night in carefree conversation. A throwback to another era.

Geoffrey was forever searching "over the rainbow" and when he penned his memoirs they were beautifully entitled *Pardon Me for Living*.

Then there was Peter Batt, more rough diamond. An East End boy who was fired from just about every newspaper in the business. A self confessed drinker and compulsive gambler, I remember during the Mexico World Cup of 1970 he had the hotel room next to me. For two days Batty lay in a drunken stupor as his newspaper desperately tried to locate him to file his copy. However as with Geoffrey Green he could write like an angel and consequently was most of the time in employment. Despite hell-raising which would have put Oliver Reid to shame, Batty became one of the first scriptwriters on EastEnders.

I must mention, too, a colleague of mine on the Daily Herald. Frank Taylor was the only sports journalist to survive the appalling Munich air disaster of February, 1958 that killed so many of Manchester United's Busby Babes. He was left with one leg three inches shorter than the other and when I knew him he wore a heavy built up boot. Frank used to always say "sometimes you must stop and smell the roses." I know why.

My first lovely daughter Sally was born while I worked Fleet Street (try telling her she's not a Geordie) and my other two equally lovely girls Deborah and Claire back home in Newcastle, though all are geographically scattered to the winds now. Including another apple of my eye, my one and only grandson Max. In all the hurly burly and bluster of a life in newspapers family must never be forgotten or overlooked – something I have learned as the years have passed and so appreciate now. Sometimes you have to smell the roses as you said Frank.

I have been extremely fortunate since I returned to the *Chron*. I've covered Newcastle United on a daily basis, reported on World Cup finals and Olympic Games in far flung locations, owned a football club, taken chat shows to places all over the North East, become a boxing agent, produced and reported on TV documentaries, and won a flurry of national Sportswriter of the Year awards.

However I fully realise that I'm not the one who is interesting, it's the people of fame I have been lucky enough to meet who hold fascination. I can now share my memories of them with you and hope you smile along with me. I've lived my professional life through them. I've been paid to do a job which is my hobby. I watch sport all over our globe from the very best seats and then get to add my own thoughts. God has been kind and it's not over yet, believe me!

SuperMac

FRIENDSHIPS ought to be unbreakable and last through many a year of famine and feast.

So it has been with Malcolm Macdonald, a centre-forward who wore Wor Jackie's mantle with such comfort.

Friends are there for one another, it's a given, and Mal was a wonderful comforter during his playing days when I lost my son Nicholas after only 11 weeks.

Many, many years later I was able to support him as his best man when Malcolm married another friend of mine Carol, once the wife of Brian Johnson, the Geordie lead singer of super group AC/DC.

We've all had some terrific nights together down the years since SuperMac swept into town as a 21-year-old chauffeured in a Rolls-Royce.

He was soccer's John Wayne, bandy legged with a swagger and enough self confidence to flood the Tyne. He was the fastest gun in the North East and just about everywhere else as it happens.

I used to ghost SuperMac's column, meeting when out of season on a Saturday morning at the Swallow Hotel, just up the road from our offices. We had our meal, did the column, and settled down to enjoy our coffee and cigars. Mal, bless him, had primed the waiter and our wine bottle never seemed to get empty.

He knew I needed to unwind after the stress of living in Shotley Bridge Hospital with a very ill Nicky and, like the good pal he is, SuperMac was ready to support without making a fuss.

That lunch went on until 10 o'clock at night as we talked about nothing and everything before I ordered a taxi and went off into the darkness. Newcastle's superstar centre-forward had given up his whole day.

You don't forget things like that and it was my joy to be Malcolm's best man when he got hitched to Carol at the Fisherman's Lodge in the grounds of Jesmond Dene.

It may have been mid June but it chucked it down all day. No matter, surrounded by family and special friends Mal and Carol had a belter of a day.

At the height of his Newcastle popularity I persuaded SuperMac and another mate of mine Rodney Bewes, he of *Likely Lads* fame, to do a couple of TV adverts for the *Chron*.

The shooting was to take place on a Sunday morning in London after United had played at Ipswich on the Saturday. Naturally to us that meant a good night out on the town. Rodney, ever the pro, wouldn't join us so Malcolm and I did as much as possible to make up for the disappointment.

Come the next morning we were like two drowned rats

while the nauseatingly healthy Bewes was jumping around bright and breezy.

To make matters worse the director decided to film the news ads featuring Bewes first and we sat around from 10am until 4pm as Rodney wanted retake after retake.

Eventually SuperMac and I were called for the soccer ad about reading Gibbo in the *Chron*. Only no one could find us... until the floor manager walked behind a piece of scenery and discovered his two potential TV stars stretched out fast asleep! I don't know if it was the fear of failure or sheer exhaustion but we completed the ad in just two takes and it couldn't have been too bad because it was part of the most successful TV campaign ever run by the *Chronicle*.

The story Malcolm loves to tell, because he can embellish it a bit at my expense, came about when he was playing in South Africa during the close season of 1975 after his great mentor Joe Harvey had quit at St James' Park.

I phoned him to break the news of the new appointment.

"Who do you think it is?" I enquired.

"Cloughie."

" No."

"Jack Charlton."

"No."

"Lawrie McMenemy."

"No."

"Don't tell me they've given it to Bob Stokoe?"

"No."

"Bloody hell, I'm running out of ideas. I give in. Who is it?"

"Gordon Lee."

"Gordon who? I've never heard of him."

It hadn't been the most auspicious of introductions between a new boss and his star player. Lee had within the first 24 hours of his appointment criticised his absent No.9 for appearing in a beer advert.

Ominously Lee added: "I'll have no stars in my team."

Now Macdonald was unquestionably a star and he knew how to handle it publicly, all of which suggested a confrontational first meeting upon SuperMac's return.

My headline 'Gordon Who?' probably only cemented the hostility felt on both sides.

Lee loved thinking footballers like Alan Gowling, a university graduate, and Graham Oates who used to sit doing the *Daily Telegraph* crossword on the team coach. Jack The Lads were most definitely out.

Gowling, an ambling, ungainly striker, was a particular favourite and Lee often would boost him at the expense of Macdonald.

One day at Stoke, Lee held an after-match Press conference and announced: "I've the best centre-forward in the country here. He should be playing for England in every match."

The tabloid hacks naturally thought he was referring to SuperMac. I knew he wasn't.

Realisation only came when, warming to his theme, Lee added: "And didn't he score a good goal today?"

Gowling had notched, Macdonald hadn't.

Jaws dropped like a boulder down a mountain side.

xxxxx

I WAS sitting in the Wembley Press box the day SuperMac made history and proved one of the country's most illustrious hacks wrong.

England were playing Cyprus in 1975 and just before kick off Brian Glanville of the *Sunday Times* was at great pains to point out to me why Macdonald would never be a true international.

Well, the game got under way and Malcolm scored one, two, three, four, FIVE goals to equal the individual scoring record for England. He knocked in every single, solitary England goal that night and if a slow smile became wider and wider with every strike adding to Glanville's discomfort then I couldn't help it. Honest!

"After my hat-trick Kevin Keegan came up and asked: 'How about making one for me?'" recalled SuperMac. "I gave him a withering look. 'Get your own ruddy goals,' I said and went off to score another two."

xxxxx

IT was a transfer dripping with history, the first Brazilian to play in the Football League in its 100-year history.

And it happened because a guy walked into Malcolm Macdonald's pub on the south coast of England offering up one Francisco Ernandi Lima da Silva. Mirandinha to thee and me.

What transpired was astonishing. SuperMac sold a new No.9 to his former Newcastle team-mate Willie McFaul and I got all the exclusive breaks on the story as it developed through my long friendship with Mal. A nice little threesome.

Out of football at the time (1988) Malcolm was running a pub in Worthing which he re-named the Far Post. A guy called Don Packham, knowing Malcolm's background, walked in, ordered a pint, and casually mentioned that through a mate in Brazil he knew a lot of Palmeiras players who wished to come to Europe. One in particular sounded tempting. Mirandinha, a centre-forward like SuperMac who possessed similar devastating pace. Bottom line, Macdonald became Mira's agent and, having failed to sell his asset to Graeme Souness at Glasgow Rangers, turned instead to his old mate McFaul, then boss of Newcastle.

When I got the inside line from SuperMac I at first treated it a little cynically but covered myself by carrying the story. However as it developed so did my excitement and the excitement of Newcastle fans.

There were bumps and grinds along the way, as there were bound to be, with people trying to cut SuperMac out of the loop. However I knew I was onto a winner before the final post loomed into sight. I flew down to Heathrow to meet Mira on his long journey from Rio de Janeiro via Paris and sit with him on the last leg of his flight to Newcastle.

That evening as he booked wearily into a city centre hotel the Brazilian flag was fluttering proudly outside and the last instalment of the Mira story was filed to the *Chronicle*.

When I did a Morecambe and Wise act with a United star

REMEMBER those hilarious Morecambe and Wise sketches where they were both sitting up in a double bed?

Not the done thing for menfolk in these days of political correctness but the one with short fat hairy legs and t'other with the horn rimmed glasses got many a laugh.

Well, I recall taking part in just such a scene with a Newcastle United footballer vaguely around that very time of Morecambe and Wise bedroom jokes.

Albert Bennett was a good mate, a chirpy chappie always ready for a giggle and a more than decent footballer who went on in retirement to become a prison warder, which presumably didn't provide the same number of laughs.

He was nicknamed Arkle because like the wonder horse he always had his ankles taped in vivid white. They were the dodgiest part of a body persistently injured, which restricted him to a mere 90 appearances (23 goals) between 1965 and 69.

However Bennett was talented enough to receive England

Under-23 honours and he fleetingly lit up the Gallowgate sky in a devastating partnership with Wyn Davies which gained United Fairs Cup qualification in season 1967/68.

Anyway, I got a bell from him this night asking if I fancied going out for a bevvy. It was midweek so all was well with the world.

We duly had a right few drinks, did a round of the hostelries and arrived back at the Bennett household where we decided upon a nightcap.

By the time all this was over we were pretty tired and rather the worse for wear so Albert suggested that, as his missus was away visiting her mother, I should stay at his place rather than attempt to find my unsteady way to Chez Gibson.

So we tumbled into the matrimonial bed and were quickly in the land of dreams. The next thing I knew was the sound of a phone ringing. A bleary-eyed Albert picked it up. I pretended I was still asleep until I heard him say: "Yes, boss. I think I've got a virus."

Suddenly I was sitting bolt upright and as I focused my gaze saw it was 11am according to the bedside clock. 11am!!! Training had well and truly been missed.

"Boss, I think it's a 24-hour virus and I haven't come in because I didn't want to pass it on to the lads," Bennett was warming to his theme.

Joe Harvey evidentally replied: "Aye, fair enough Albert. Stay warm. See you in the morning." Just as Bennett was about to hang up Joe added: "Albert, Albert, whatever you do say nowt to the Press."

On another occasion when United were staying in

Blackpool a few of the lads, including Bennett and myself, slipped out for a breath of fresh air. Before we knew where we were we ended up in a nightclub run by Colin 'Tiny' Prince. Colin, built like the side of a mountain, had starred on *The One O'Clock Show*, a daily programme on Tyne Tees Television which is why we popped in.

The place was packed and we were standing at the back having a beer. I glanced down and there was a huge rock pool with what looked like small alligators motionless in it.

I said to Albert: "Bet they're real."

"Naw," he replied, "but I'll find out." With that he put his leg over the two-foot rail round the pool and smacked this little alligator on its snout with the steel capped heel of his boot. Honest, even my eyes watered.

This thing suddenly recoiled its tail in pain and a mini tidal wave of water shot past us and drenched the beehive hairstyle of the young ladies sitting with their backs to us. They looked like candyfloss after a rain storm.

Talk about chaos but by the time they turned round like drowned rats to see what had happened we had taken to our toes.

xxxxx

WHEN I was a young buck in flairs and velvet jacket, a visit to the Football Writers Association dinner in London 48 hours before the FA Cup final was the perfect way to kick off an end-of-season party. I was there every year with various Newcastle players as my guests.

Well this particular time Ian La Frenais, the Geordie creator of *The Likely Lads* and *Auf Wiedersehen, Pet*, was with me and we fell into the company of Rod Stewart, a football freak.

Come chucking out time Rod grandly invited us all back to his hotel suite for a sherbet or two. He was romancing the delicious Britt Ekland and said he would just give her a call as a warning.

Rod sheepishly returned a few minutes later to say, er, the party was off. Britt had evidently told him no way were drunken footballers and hacks descending on her domain and he had better get himself home.

It was a joy to see that even one of the world's great lotharios got his comeuppance now and again.

xxxxx

A GLORIOUS lap of honour had been completed with the tulip-shaped European Fairs Cup held triumphantly aloft in the Budapest summer night air.

As I forced my way downstairs towards United's dressing-room to continue the celebrations I turned the corner and there was Benny Arentoft, one of Newcastle's three goalscorers, on the phone still in his full strip with sweat pouring down his face.

He nodded looking a bit sheepish as I disappeared through the door for a glass of champagne to be thrust into my hand.

A short while later Arentoft appeared to join in the fun.

"What was that all about?" I inquired.

It turned out Benny was working for a Danish newspaper and filing a report on the final. Wonder how he described his own equaliser that took the game beyond Ujpest Dozsa!

Can you imagine Wayne Rooney reporting for the *Manchester Evening News* or Steven Gerrard writing a match report for the *Liverpool Echo*? No, neither can I.

He was quite a character was Preben. He worked as an accountant for Copenhagen Council, played as an amateur with Bronshoj, gained a shock transfer to Scotland of all places to join Greenock Morton, married a Scottish girl, and ended up over the border at Newcastle at a time when foreigners were still a novelty in this country.

XXXXX

RAY KING was a goalkeeper for Newcastle United during the forties when Wor Jackie and Stan Seymour were shaping a squad which would triumph at Wembley in the FA Cup final three times in the blink of an eye.

Born in Amble, Ray never lasted long enough to become part of the black and whites of the Fab Fifties but was a more than decent keeper who became a legend with Port Vale and played for England B.

King eventually returned home to Amble where one day he was addressing the local schoolkids about being a Magpie. One cheeky little nipper piped up: "How old are you, Mr King?"

"Eighty two lad," came the reply.

"Oh," said a shocked looking pupil, "I wouldn't want to be that old."

"You will, son, when you're 81," smiled Ray.

XXXXX

BILL McGARRY was brought in as manager of United to kill the player power that had blossomed under out-of-his-depth boss Richard Dinnis.

The board wanted what they perceived as the troublemakers cleaned out and felt hardman McGarry was the perfect executioner.

The only trouble was that McGarry couldn't build a side as easily as he could smash one. Second Division fodder was the food of the day and inevitably the man took the chop.

When he did McGarry called an impromptu Press conference. Staring directly at me he declared: "You got me the sack!"

"Thank you, Mr McGarry," I replied. "That's the nicest thing you've ever said to me."

Meeting Grace's little boy

GRACE KELLY was the original ice cool blonde. A Hollywood goddess renowned for her elegance and style, with just a hint of red blooded passion beneath a beautifully serene surface.

Every man who was not already besotted with the more basic sexuality of Marilyn Monroe hankered after Her Graciousness.

So to meet her son face to face and spend an hour alone in his company was not just a special thrill but something of a coup. It doesn't happen to us ordinary Geordie lads.

Oh, I should mention her son is Prince Albert of Monaco, then the heir to the throne and now firmly ensconced upon it.

I was unexpectedly granted an exclusive audience with Prince Albert when Newcastle United played Monaco in the quarter-final of the UEFA Cup in March of 1997.

It took place at the Gosforth Park Hotel when Monaco flew over for the first leg. A guard stood on the door of a bar cleared to allow only myself and the Prince inside. Quite a moment for my memoirs.

Albert was a devout disciple of the principality's football club, bearing a love of our national sport which doesn't afflict the Queen or Duke of Edinburgh. He flew over for what was to be a momentous night of success for the tiniest but most wealthy of acreages.

A Newcastle businessman who I knew in my youth was responsible for pulling off the impossible. Joe Robertson is a Geordie who made his pile here and then hot-footed it to play in Monaco. I knew Joe well, he claimed to be a friend of Prince Albert, and casually asked if I would like an exclusive interview when Monaco came over to town. Amazingly he delivered.

The exclusive was blazed across the back page of the *Chron*, then a broadsheet, on March 4 under the headline "My Euro dream by the real Prince Albert" (as opposed to Philippe Albert!)

The heir to the throne talked knowledgeably about football and his beloved team with not a hint of superiority or arrogance. He revealed that he first watched Monaco at the age of five or six when his father, Prince Rainier, took him.

"I was hooked," he told me adding: "This is the best team we've had in the last decade. We had great teams in the 60s and 80s but this one is special."

Indeed it was. Boasting such fine future stars of the Premier League as Thierry Henry, Emmanuel Petit and Fabien Barthez, they easily took care of Newcastle in a season in which they would also claim the French championship.

Albert spoke openly of Monaco's lasting problem, a chronic lack of support at the turnstiles.

"We have only 30,000 people and a catchment area of 55,000," he shrugged. "We can't expect people to come from Cannes or Nice because they have their own teams.

"We've tried many things to increase attendances but football isn't the only game in town. People take their families skiing at weekends."

I know, we have the same problem in Wallsend and Newbiggin Hall!

What perhaps wasn't realised is that Albert was a top sportsman himself. Apart from playing football regularly with his well-heeled mates he actually took part in three Winter Olympics as part of Monaco's bobsleigh team.

"I have to train almost the whole year long," he told me, "and that's time-consuming with my royal commitments.

"I got interested in the sport through skiing – I was persuaded to take my first bobsleigh driving course in St Moritz in 1986 and another a few months later in Austria.

"From that I helped form the federation and, I like to think, increase the awareness of bobsleighing within Monaco."

Of course he touched upon his mam Princess Grace and talked of her with great affection, then it was time to go. A firm handshake, a smile of warmth and a "farewell, I may see you tonight" and Prince Albert vanished. The bar returned to normal service.

My links with Monaco began immediately after the draw when the *Chron* decided to send me out to the principality to tell of its uniqueness. It's an idyllic place which has turned the world on its head: no slums, no real poverty, no crime.

Money is god and billionaires stand cheek to jowl on its gold plated pavements.

Joe Robertson met us – me and a snapper – and whisked us on a tour of the grand and the grander. We sat outside the world famous casino where I interviewed Monaco's playmaker John Collins, used to the passion of Glasgow Celtic but now playing in the Stade Louis II stadium where two's a crowd.

Bathing in the sun, shades on for effect, John was anxious to get the official chat out of the way so he could regale me with his love of Newcastle.

"I held my stag night in the Bigg Market," he told me proudly. "I love Newcastle and used to come down regularly. Many's the time I have stood at the Gallowgate end of St James' Park with my mates. I know United were in for me once but Celtic were asking silly money."

The money isn't silly in Monaco. It's plentiful.

I loved every minute of my association with Monaco – except for the two matches both won by the French club, 1-0 here and 3-0 there.

However the highlight of it all was spending an hour with Grace Kelly's little lad!

xxxxx

WHEN I was working on one of my books – *United Behind The Headlines* – I was given exclusive access to those within St James' Park because of my involvement with the Magpie Group that had delivered Kevin Keegan and his Entertainers to a grateful Tyneside.

Most of the yarns were about Keegan's extraordinary signings, and one of the stories I liked best I persuaded Freddy Shepherd to tell on record. It was when United capped all by going over to Italy and signing Tino Asprilla, as colourful as a rainbow.

A complicated deal was done with Parma at £7.5m but when United's medical people started making noises about Tino's knee – the worry was about deterioration setting in – the Italians were convinced the Mags were trying to pull out of the transfer.

Shep recalled with a chortle. "We sent two of our top men, Freddie Fletcher and Russell Jones, over to Italy as peacemakers.

"At the end of tricky talks the Parma president said a few words in Italian and our lads replied, 'Thank you very much', shaking hands in turn.

"A bemused interpreter asked, "Why do you shake hands? He just called you little s***s'."

xxxxx

MIKE MAHONEY Super Goalie (as the supporters' ditty went) lived just round the corner from me in Whickham.

We used to visit the local hostelries midweek for a jar or two. Just to be sociable you understand.

He was good company was Mick, a ringer for one of *The Wurzels* with his Bristol burr except that it was all topped off by a Noddy Holder hair set. After keeping goal for United in the 1976 League Cup final at Wembley, Mahoney went off to chance his arm in America as other Mags such as

Paul Cannell and Rocky Hudson did. So when I was due to cover the 1994 World Cup finals in the States I got in touch with Mick.

His wanderings had seen him end up in Los Angeles where he was driving a truck. As the World Cup final was in LA it was obvious we should meet up. Big mistake. I had given up smoking for a whole year but Mahoney still had a chimney on top of his head.

He came over and kipped on the floor of my hotel room. At four o'clock in the morning having made a valiant effort to clear the bar I reached across and took a fag out of his packet. One wouldn't make much difference. Oh yeah? One became five, became 10, became 20.

Before long I was on a 50-a-day habit (yes, honestly). Luckily I managed to give up completely eight or nine years ago and without MM on hand to tempt me I have survived dastardly-weed clear.

Mind you Mahoney's closer now, having returned here to live in Devon, and he was up for a Joe Harvey memorial night when we shared a late-night hotel once again but this time without me being Fag Ash Lil.

When I was James Bond behind the Iron Curtain

WE WERE supposed to be partying in celebration of one of the most auspicious days in Newcastle United's global existence.

The Magpies were on the River Danube preparing for their European Fairs Cup final second leg against crack Hungarians Ujpest Dozsa.

The tulip-shaped silver pot was but an hour and a half from landing in Geordie hands and the celebrations had already begun.

We had been invited to the British Embassy for drinks and nibbles, the official recognition of the success of a northerly city in the competitive arena of sport.

However this was significantly different and, innocents abroad, we were about to be plunged into a world of espionage and intrigue where James Bond may well have been secreted just round the next murky corner.

This was Budapest, behind the Iron Curtain and capital of a country crushed by Russian tanks. It was 1969, just 13 years after the brutal overthrow of the Hungarian Uprising.

The Cold War still existed, not like today. The fictitious Iron Curtain wasn't dismantled until 1989 and several buildings we passed in Budapest still carried bullet scars from the bloody battle which claimed the lives of 2,500 Hungarians and 700 Soviet troops.

This was far from our thoughts, however, as we enjoyed the light-hearted chatter in the Embassy and then, as our time had obviously elapsed, the signal came that we ought to head for the exit. Casually a couple of the girls and fellas asked if we would like to go on and have an impromptu party at their place. Of course we would. The night was young and so were we.

It was mainly hacks who agreed. The players weren't involved. They were locked up in their hotel set amongst the beautiful parkland of Margaret Island, slap bang in the middle of the Danube. They had serious business to do.

We piled into a couple of official cars and sped through the Budapest streets where no doubt fighting had in 1956 been full frontal.

The mood was light and fun. More patter than a fortnight's rain.

However when we drew up to the kerb and got out we were discreetly pulled to one side.

"Just to let you know, it might be a good idea if we didn't discuss anything political or about the uprising once we're inside," a pretty slip of a girl informed us.

Why? "Well, we know the house is bugged which means the Soviets will be listening in. We don't want to give them anything to latch onto do we?" Excuse me, am I hearing right? Have we just been warned that our party is bugged? Had our hosts waited until we were outside because the cars were bugged too?

"Oh, we know everything is bugged," came the reply matter of factly. "We sweep the place periodically, find the hidden recorders, and get rid of them. Then they come along shortly afterwards and place listening devices somewhere different. It's a bit of a game really!"

A bit of a game? When we first got inside we could hardly drink our spirits for wondering what lurked behind the big pictures on the walls.

At one stage I discovered a member of our Press pack staring wide-eyed at a huge mirror while bragging loud and clear about how Newcastle were going to stuff the Hungarians the next night. I bet that worried Moscow!

Of course United did the business. Three-nil victory at home, 3-2 win away and the job was a good 'un.

xxxxx

FAIRS CUP winning boss Joe Harvey possessed two major assets that went a long way to guaranteeing success – his man-management and his uncanny ability to scout talent.

Harvey might have looked blue jawed and capable of chewing girders like Desperate Dan but he had a way with words which stood him in excellent stead.

Whether defusing a situation or lifting the spirits of his troops, Harvey was a wily old operator who could pick the right words. Not flowery, often very basic, but with just the right effect.

Like when, having done what he was brought back to do –
win promotion to the old First Division – he was preparing
for United's very first game in the top flight. It was against
Nottingham Forest at St James' Park.

The bell had gone meaning it was time to take the field
and the players rose, a couple bouncing a ball, others kicking
the wall with their boots. "Hey, just a minute lads," said Joe.
Pause. "Remember, whatever you do, don't let them panic
you into playing football!"

Laughter everywhere. The tension, the pressure of a big
match at home evaporated. Game on.

Joe's most famous speech, of course, was delivered at
half-time in the European Fairs Cup final in Budapest when
a 3-0 home lead had been drastically cut by two first-half
Ujpest goals.

The door burst open and in blew Harvey to face his
troops, slumped on the dressing-room benches.

"What's the matter with you?" Joe boomed. "They're
bloody foreigners. Score a goal and their bottle will go."

Bob Moncur did score early on. Ujpest's bottle did go.
And it was Wor Cup. Joe was 50 that very day. With tears
welling in his eyes, Harvey sat wreathed in smiles as the
players sang "happy birthday, dear gaffer!" Europe was an
exciting roller-coaster ride. A new experience we all gobbled
up with relish.

A number of us Press lads used to make the spying trips
with Harvey as soon after the draw was announced as
possible. I say spying trips but in reality they were little more
than a promotional exercise.

When United drew the mighty Inter Milan off we went

again, this time to Lake Como, breathtaking in its beauty. It was a cup-tie and Inter were the royal visitors.

Programmes were a rarity in Continental football and I made my way to the dressing rooms to get the Inter team before taking my seat next to Harvey. Throughout the match Joe, smoking fag after fag, cracked jokes and never once made a note or asked a player's name. These highly technical days managers inevitably carry book and pen when striding the technical area ready for their pearls of wisdom at half-time.

After the cup tie Harvey came out with enough emotive quotes to satisfy my sports editor back in Newcastle and, mission over, we returned to Tyneside.

A couple of weeks later we flew out to Milan for the first leg and, on the morning of the match while I was still filing my copy to the office, there was a loud banging on my bedroom door. It was Joe.

"Bloody hell, Gibbo, have you still got a copy of Inter Milan's team from Como?" he asked with some urgency. "We've got a team meeting and I've got to tell the lads something about their lot."

Sounds daft, doesn't it? Even comical. But Joe was no fool. He passionately believed his team ought to concentrate on what they wanted to do and let the opposition worry about them. He didn't fill the players' heads with fear or hand out detailed dossiers which would inevitably send them to sleep if they were read at all.

"It'll be all right on the night," Joe used to say and usually it was! Oh, and to prove the point, United drew with Inter in the San Siro and beat them in the return at St James' Park.

Top footballer on thirty quid a week

IT BECAME a routine – after a match on a Saturday we would find our way down to Roy's Two Rooms for a snifter and to right the wrongs of that afternoon's work.

It was a restaurant no more than a goalkeeper's punt from the Gallowgate End of St James' Park where Roy Santos and singer Johnny Heenan would look after us with relish.

We had our own Rat Pack and the night would stretch into the early hours. This particular evening Paul Cannell was one of the clan.

Handsome with black flowing hair and a moustache, Paul looked as though he had just stepped off one of those cigarette cards of old Hollywood film stars.

Cannell didn't take a walk on the wild side. He lived there permanently. Anyway, I congratulated him on a good goalscoring performance.

"Aye, Gibbo," he replied, "but I'm still only paid thirty quid a week!" How much? Paul had only just broken into the side but he was notching, this was the seventies not Wor Jackie's fifties, and the money was paltry. Flabbergasted, I eventually asked if I could print the fact and Cannell cheerily said I could. He felt it might emphasise that not every footballer was getting fortunes.

A few of the players used to go down to the Eldon Grill for a pint after training on Mondays and of course Paul was front of the queue.

A mate joined them and said: "Hey, have you seen that? A Newcastle player is only on thirty quid." Suddenly Cannell felt somewhat uneasy.

He told me afterwards: "I naively thought the story would only get a bit on the back page but it was splashed on page one and every placard in town blazed the words: 'United star on £30 a week'."

What was the outcome? Well, Cannell didn't get the rollicking some thought he might. Instead United got in touch directly with me for a follow-up! "For the first time ever Newcastle revealed a player's wage slip in detail," recalled Paul smiling. "They listed by appearance money and win bonus which made the overall figure look much better of course, but my basic WAS £30 a week."

All's well that ends well of course, and shortly afterwards Cannell got a significant rise on his basic. Job done.

Cannell, a local lad from Heaton, was a decent centre-forward who scored 19 goals in 69 matches for United before going off to play in America, which was ideally suited to his rock 'n roll lifestyle.

His main club was Washington Diplomats although he enjoyed a few jaunts round the major cities. Naturally

Paul quickly discovered the best watering holes, in this case Winston's in the Georgetown party area of Washington.

As usual he pulled a pretty young lady, danced, and made arrangements to see her again.

The following morning, slightly hungover, Cannell got a call from the Diplomats' PR department.

"What the hell were you up to in Winston's last night?" he was asked.

"Nowt special," he replied.

"Nothing special? You only made a date with the President's daughter!"

Ouch, the young lady was Susan Ford.

xxxxx

HOW often is European club football played on New Year's Day?

It isn't ideal but we first footed in Spain on the way to Fairs Cup success as 1968 gave way to '69.

Driving my car gingerly into St James' Park it still wasn't light. The snow, six inches deep after days of drifting, was beginning to melt and the slush made it difficult to get up the incline and round to the main car park.

Our worst fears were confirmed when director James Rush, once a squadron leader, arrived to tell us that Newcastle Airport was closed. Our chartered Viscount had to be diverted to Middleton Saint George for pick-up.

It was with a sense of relief that we flew over the snow-capped Pyrenees, a breathtaking sight, and swept down into the cathedral city of Zaragoza, deep in Spain's northern territory. Joe Harvey's problem was how to handle New Year's Eve in the Goya Hotel. He decided not to fight tradition and actually allowed United's players to fleetingly take part in the Ceremony of the Grapes even though they were playing the following day.

Granada, a Spanish First Division side, were staying with us before playing a friendly. Hence they stayed up while United's players hit the hay a tad late. In our honour a couple of Granada footballers donned Beatles wigs and sang lustily, finishing off by chanting "New-cas-el, New-cas-el". We quickly caught the mood, responding with our version of Granada.

Oh, the game? United lost 3-2 but with only a deficit of one goal and a couple of away strikes in the back pocket it was all right.

Afterwards my concern was to file copy back to Newcastle as quickly as possible and then join the team for better-late-than-never celebrations. However I was tipped off that something interesting was happening in the hotel foyer so I sneaked downstairs. There were two burly, pistol packing Spanish cops in agitated conversion with Jim Scott and coach Dave Smith. Eventually United's interpreter was called and passports were carefully examined.

It turned out that the police were looking for two Englishmen called Scott and Smith who had absconded from custody and they were convinced United's pair were the guilty men.

"I wouldn't care but two canny Scots being taken for English men is what really hurts," moaned Smith.

Cracking stuff. Another story winged itself across to the

Chron offices and made a page one exclusive: United Pair In Police Swoop.

XXXXX

BILLY WHITEHURST was frightening. Both as a centre-forward who made Desperate Dan look like Liberace and as a drinking companion on a night out.

Driving into a brick wall had less impact.

Here was a hellraiser with the kick of a mule. I drank with him and I listened to those who occupied the same pitch like Glenn Roeder.

"I used to go to Brough Park dogs with Big Billy," Glenn told me. "Shortly after he left Newcastle we had to go and play his new club Oxford. I was taking no chances. All I did all game was talk to Billy about Brough. To keep on the right side of him because friendship would count for nothing in the heat of battle."

United's other central defender Peter Jackson wasn't so crafty. He got his nose smashed across his face.

"Jacko didn't have the sense of Glenn," explained Whitehurst when I spoke to him a couple of years later. "We used to have a few battles when he was at Bradford in the old Second and Third Divisions. He fancied himself as a bit of a hardman but he wasn't in my league.

"Jacko tried to rough me up so I splattered him. Broke his nose. Lesson learned."

When Big Bad Billy phoned me up upon signing for Sunderland after leaving the Mags to announce "I'm back", my heart sank as well as soared. I knew I was to face another Becher's Brook. Whitehurst virtually finished the international career of Paul Bracewell at St James' Park on New Year's Day in 1986. Brace didn't play again for almost two years after a bone-shuddering confrontation with Billy that rearranged his ankle.

Usually Whitehurst would accept the blame with a shrug of his huge shoulders but he has always maintained that he didn't do Bracewell, merely met him head on.

There's no question the highly talented midfielder saw it differently. Anyway they met up again when Brace was assistant manager at Sunderland.

"I played for both Sunderland and Sheffield United so I went to see them play one another on Wearside," recalled Billy. "I admit I'd had a few drinks and after the game, which Sunderland lost 4-1, I was half cut, went into their dressing room, took off all my clothes, and jumped in the bath. Bracewell was sitting in the other end and he leapt out like a shot and was away. He wasn't having any of it."

When I thought I would die with Bjorn Borg

BJORN BORG was the matinee idol of the tennis courts. A cool Swede with long flowing hair who sent the girls into ecstasy.

Oh, and he was the most successful tennis player on Planet Earth, which rather helped the sale of the Borg image.

Back in June of 1980 Newcastle was a city amid the trumpeting of great celebration for its 900th anniversary and it was decided that to bring Borg here just days before he went on to win his fifth Wimbledon singles title would be something of a coup.

Car manufacturers Saab, being a Swedish company, were wildly enthusiastic about backing the project and as part of the much-wanted publicity it was decided they would fly me down to London to link up with Borg and accompany him back to Newcastle, with me telling the story of undiluted joy in the *Chron*.

No one, however, could foresee what a dramatic yarn it would turn out to be.

While I slept in my comfy hotel bed overnight, the weather took a distinct turn for the worse and by the time curtains were opened I was greeted by gale force winds and whipping rain.

So much so that our regular flight north was cancelled and we had to journey across London to a small airfield and board a private plane.

All very nice except that these planes are tiny compared to a jet and the weather was wild.

No sooner had we lifted off than the aircraft was buffeted incessantly and began dropping up to a 60 feet a time like a boulder tossed down a well.

Borg, Mr Cool, was as white as a sheet and visibly shaking and I could hear the pilot sitting just in front of me exchanging messages that were, shall we say, not gauged to increase confidence. I decided it was time to panic.

In due course we were told that Newcastle Airport was closed and we should divert to Teesside.

"No," said our trusty pilot with Douglas Bader bravado, "we're coming in. I have a celebrity passenger and we're an hour late already."

By now my mind was running riot. I recalled when Buddy Holly died in a plane crash. I'd just seen him and The Crickets live in Newcastle. The question was who died with him? The Big Bopper? Yeah, yeah, I remember *Chantilly Lace*, a great song. Ritchie Valens? Anyone else? I could see myself being a quiz question. Honest!

Who died with Bjorn Borg? Some local hack wasn't it? A quick glance at Bjorn didn't help. John McEnroe never scared him like this.

Eventually we made it, only just, and walked through Eldon Square to a pop star welcome for the man by my side.

Borg told me later that he had always hated flying, "especially in small private planes that can be buffeted so easily." I would never have guessed.

Of course the story made the front page of the *Chron* on the Monday (we flew in Saturday).

A week later the world No.1, still only 24 years of age, defended his Wimbledon crown by overpowering the Superbrat McEnroe 1-6, 7-5, 6-3, 6-7, 8-6 in what was hailed as a classic final.

Cool and confident under fire, I marvelled at Borg's performance and contrasted it greatly with the jibbering guy who sat next to me on a journey into hell. It was the same Bjorn Borg, wasn't it?

xxxxx

SOME time ago Glenn McCrory and I decided to make a documentary entitled *The Meanest Man On Earth*.

It all came about because of a long conversation we had over a bottle of ruby red. I was citing the case for Sonny Liston, who I had actually met and spent some time with, and Glenn was backing Mike Tyson, who he had sparred with as a young fighter on his way up.

We decided to film in Las Vegas (flash weren't we?) because that's where I met Liston, where he lived, died and is buried. Besides we had a couple of quid expenses from Tyne Tees Television after winning a prize for the most inventive idea for a documentary.

Both Liston and Tyson were world heavyweight champions who could curdle milk at 50 paces, such were their fearsome personas.

Donkey's years earlier I had been over in Vegas staying at the Thunderbird Hotel, where Liston used to train, and had lunch with him. Throughout he stared down at the table with chilling menace, occasionally grunting some sort of answer to our conversation.

I had a snapper coming in and wanted to record my moment of history with the baddest guy around – only when the camera appeared Sonny went all sunny with a melon smile and a snuggle up to his 'mate.' Me.

The next day when I was walking through one of the countless casinos on the strip I saw Liston approaching. Interesting, I thought. Will he bother to recognise me?

Indeed he did but when his wife showed little interest (and why should she?) he gave her such a backhander and growled "Speak to the man!" that I didn't know whether to stick or twist.

When I went back with McCrory we visited Liston's grave on the flight path of the great jumbos flying in the next load of gamblers to be fleeced. His resting place is in the Davis Memorial Gardens of Peace and is marked only by the words "Charles Sonny Liston, A Man." And what a man!

As for Tyson, eloquently backed by Glenn, I have met him since and got the same sunny disposition that Liston afforded me. What is it with these bone crushers? Underneath do they want to be known as Mr Nice Guy?

We did a talk in together in Newcastle and, though on the short side for a heavyweight, that tattoo on his face only made Tyson appear even more menacing. I was warned that he could be moody and difficult yet he was anything but.

We sat together in an ante room and on the top table and he was full of tales and jokes. After our hour long session Tyson grabbed me in a big bear hug and planted a huge smacker on my forehead.

Mind you, I kept my ears well out of range just in case. I've also worked with Evander Holyfield and saw what Mike had done to him.

The crazy world of Gazza

PAUL GASCOIGNE was the footballing icon of the nineties, the boy who was "daft as a brush" according to his England manager Bobby Robson yet sparked Gazzamania at the 1990 World Cup finals which changed his life forever.

A Geordie with an impish sense of humour and a heart of pure gold, he was a clown with a tear never far from the corner of his eye.

The greatest English footballing genius of his generation, Gazza was equally tormented by injuries and demons. It was said that Stella Artois became his girlfriend as he self-destructed in an orgy of booze, drugs, pain and the mind-gripping obsessive compulsive disorder.

Maybe, but one thing always shone through the confusion. Gazza was a ruddy brilliant footballer. And he was totally, wonderfully ours. All ours.

I've known Paul throughout his long and colourful journey, from a fresh faced cheeky kid receiving a trophy from me at the local social club, through his great years when I visited him at his luxury villa in Rome, on to late in his playing days when he magnificently came riding to my rescue in helping raise funds to save Gateshead, his hometown football club. Through dentist chairs, broken hearts, and futile redemption.

I have a treasure chest full of happy memories and they are the ones I prefer to concentrate on at the expense of the more lurid. That he now stands on the brink of a dark abyss is little short of a tragedy.

He was still nowt more than a bairn when United created history by signing the first ever Brazilian to play in the Football League.

The rest of the players reckoned Mirandinha and Gazza needed a ball apiece such was their obsession with it. "Mira wouldn't pass me the salt," moaned Paul.

They argued like crazy on the pitch but off it were hilarious.

Mira was the forerunner of what has since become the norm – a Newcastle player who could hardly speak English. But then neither could Gazza!

What Paul told Mira to say to young ladies on the Tuxedo Princess floating nightclub when meeting them cannot be repeated in a family publication.

I had them on stage together more than once round the social clubs of the North East. Gazza reckoned his goldfish looked like Mira with his mouth open. Mira called Gazza "the crazy one."

One night at Ponteland Social Club Paul ended the session by sitting down at the organ on the stage and belting out rock 'n' roll numbers like Little Richard. How the audience loved him.

Gazza was totally unpredictable, sometimes infuriating, but always fun. I once arranged to pick him up at Jesmond Tennis Club to do a chat show in Ashington. I emphasised the time and the importance of not keeping the audience waiting and Gazza said: "Aye, not to worry."

When I walked through the gate there was Paul still on court playing mixed doubles. He winked, won a couple of points to tie up the match, and ran across with sweat pouring off him. Inevitably he had left his suit back home in Dunston which meant a trip across town for him to get changed.

He drove like someone demented, waving cheerily to everyone on every street corner until we made it to his house. Upstairs he ran about shouting to his mam for his newly ironed shirt, only to discover that his dad had put it on and gone off to the pub.

Eventually Gazza emerged to inform me that we would have to go round to his girlfriend's – he had left the jacket of his suit there the night before.

By now I was bordering on hysteria but Gazza was as happy-go-lucky as a punter with the pools up. The drive to Ashington seemed to take an eternity and we were met outside the club by a bunch of harassed officials looking in desperation for any sign of their lost performers.

We went on stage in front of a fidgety audience well over an hour late, but Paul soon charmed them with a succession of daft tales about how he booked a sunbed course for black centre-forward Tony Cunningham. It's hard to be angry at the lack of political correctness when you're laughing!

Mind you, there was a sensitive side to the young clown. We did a gig at Morpeth with Paul Goddard and as usual Gazza had them in stitches until, right at the death, a punter asked a question about money supposedly offered to Paul to stay at Newcastle.

"I'm an out of work miner who spends all my dole money to watch you on a Saturday," he said with feeling. "Yet you turn down £2,000 a week to stay at the club."

Gazza answered quickly, I wrapped the show up, and we were off stage. At the reception in the back room Gazza went missing and with a queue of fans waiting for autographs I set off looking for him. He was locked in a toilet cubicle with tears rolling down his cheeks.

The realisation that a fan could think a working class lad like himself was too big for his boots destroyed him. I had to wipe away the tears with a piece of toilet paper and help him pull himself together before he could come out to face his admirers.

Gascoigne inevitably followed Chris Waddle and Peter Beardsley out of Newcastle as they sold their Geordie gems and predictably got relegated. When he finally moved again, this time to Lazio, I arranged to go out and see him. Geordie meets Geordie in La Dolce Vita – not the nightclub in Newcastle but Rome sweet Rome.

The *Chron* had booked me into a hotel but Paul was having none of it. He moved me into his villa where I lived not only for the duration of my stay but three extra days after being persuaded by him to take in the weekend and Lazio's match against Napoli.

Gazza was obsessed by motorbikes – he had no fewer than nine Harley-Davidsons at one stage. However Lazio, realising their prize asset was a tile short of a roof, banned him from driving to training on his power machine.

So what did our Geordie jester do? Donned a German Second World War helmet, drove through the choking Rome traffic like a maniac with his dad and me in a vehicle behind him, parked his bike in a garage just round the corner from Lazio's training ground, leaped into our car, and arrived all sweetness and light.

On the way home Gazza would flick a switch to electronically open the gates to his villa, roar up the long driveway straight through the open patio windows, park his Harley-Davidson on the sheepskin rug, take off his German helmet to plonk himself in an armchair and watch Elvis videos!

Mad as a butcher's dog, he got up in the middle of the night one time, wakened me, and sneaked off to a nearby bedroom where one of his mates from Newcastle was sleeping. Meticulously Gazza shaved off one of his eyebrows.

xxxxx

I SPENT 11 years as owner of Gateshead FC which seemed a life sentence at times, pure joy on other occasions.

Anyway we hit massive financial problems when our main sponsor pulled out mid season and I unashamedly called on my friends in football to help bail us out.

Alan Shearer did a talk-in free of charge at St James' Park and Gazza, a Gateshead lad, fronted a sporting dinner for nowt. He sold out 750 tickets at 30-odd quid a head in 24 hours, such was his pulling power, despite all that was happening around him.

Of course I got 'the treatment.' When my back was turned as I made an announcement on the mike, Paul would move in. Peppering my steak, spiking my drink, and generally causing chaos, all to the amusement of the watching punters.

Of course it was childish but it was pure Gazza and, bless him, I didn't mind one little bit. I knew what was going on just as a dad knows what his kid is up to but still plays the game.

During the build up to the dinner date Gazza had got Stan Ternent, his manager at Burnley and a fellow Geordie, to give me a bell at the *Chron*. "John Gibson? I'm Stan Ternent, I believe you have Gazza up next week for a dinner. I'm afraid he won't be able to make it. It's international week as you know and I'm taking all the players away to Spain for warm weather training."

I almost burst a blood vessel… until I heard guffawing in the background. Gazza had asked his boss to set me up as a joke.

Both Gazza and Stan were top table and Gateshead were saved.

xxxxx

I ALWAYS remember Kevin Keegan banging on about taking German lessons after he had signed for Hamburg, where he was twice voted European Footballer of the Year.

KK reckoned his willingness to embrace German culture

was the cornerstone of his success. And he advised Gazza to do likewise upon moving to Lazio.

I could understand why. Gazza spoke Geordie, not English, and that presumably could be a problem in a city of culture. However, getting Gazza to night school was never going to work so I presumed that he was a lost cause.

Imagine my surprise then during my stay at his Rome villa to hear Paul greet the little kids seeking his autograph and their dads seeking his favours with a warm response in their native tongue. Pigeon Italian it may have been, but it was impressive and well appreciated by the locals.

When we drove to a Lazio home game the cheering fans, spotting their hero, thrust their Lazio scarves through the window of our vehicle until we were knee deep in them. I still have a few in the back of my wardrobe as a souvenir of a memorable stay with a madcap Geordie.

When I took a Rolls-Royce trip round London with showbiz stars

THE dark, gleaming Rolls-Royce purred down Fulham Road with stereophonic pop bouncing from a tape recorder to add to an air of opulence that even stretched to electronically operated windows. This was the Swinging Sixties.

Sitting in the back were Bob Moncur, Willie McFaul and coach Dave Smith. I was in the front next to a young man with flowing locks, handsome features and a burning passion to write which had brought him his Roller and a hundred other things, and to watch his beloved football team.

Ian La Frenais, Geordie despite his surname, was an immensely talented young film and TV writer who had, along with his backseat passengers, been my guests at the Football Writers' Association dinner within the elegant Cafe Royal where the Player of the Year was duly crowned. Actor Tom Courtenay was another of our original party but sadly he was having to do a television interview instead of the town.

This could have been any year of a dozen or more. Traditionally at midnight FWA members and guests began to leave the Cafe Royal and drift out to swell the hundreds who haunt London's swish nightspots.

Under the expert guidance of La Frenais we used to do just that. Both footballers and showbiz personalities are drawn together like moths to a light and revel in one another's company.

Through Ian, who created the *Likely Lads* and later *Auf Wiedersehen, Pet* amongst a glittering array of credits, I was rubbing shoulders with showbiz stars every time United played in London.

I dined with the likes of Ian McShane (*Lovejoy*) whose father used to play for Manchester United, Michael Crawford, Tom Courtenay, Roman Polanski (before his troubles) and of course Rodney Bewes of *Likely Lads* stardom who became a good pal.

Before one visit to London to play Chelsea at Stamford Bridge just prior to Christmas La Frenais decided he wanted to do something special.

Then it hit him: a private film show for United's players and manager Joe Harvey on the Friday night before the match. The only snag was that United always caught the six o'clock train to London, getting in around 10.30pm before going straight to bed.

However, the idea of a special film show in their honour appealed to the lads and the club relaxed, agreeing to let them go on the one o'clock train which got in town at tea time.

That week Ian was never off the phone telling me what

he had arranged. He went to colossal bother to make it a great night out.

Ian somehow picked up a film of United's 1911 FA Cup final against Bradford City and the 1951 Wembley win over Blackpool to run as an appetiser to a full-length showing of Kelly's Heroes.

"Don't tell Joe," demanded our host, "it'll be a surprise for him."

A fleet of taxis picked us up at the Great Northern Hotel outside King's Cross and whisked us through Soho's narrow, thronged streets to Royalty House, where Ian was waiting to greet us. Inside, sitting quietly tucked away at the back, was Rodney Bewes.

Later that night after the players had gone back to their hotel for an early night's sleep and we had ventured out for a meal, Rodney turned up his lapel to reveal a Chelsea supporter's badge.

"I felt as a mark of respect that I shouldn't flaunt it in front of the opposition," he smiled.

The lads had a howl when they saw Joe Harvey in his long baggy shorts and massive shin guards playing at an apparently slow pace. However didn't he have the last laugh when at the end of the film the camera closed in on him being held shoulder high with the cup gripped in his hands.

"Try doing that, you lot," whooped Harvey.

La Frenais treasured the evening, gaining the same schoolboy pleasure that he had enjoyed when I first took him in to the St James' Park Press box and he saw the great Jackie Milburn sitting right there in front of him. Ian told me he often used to gaze at the half dome on the top of the stand as a kid and wonder what the scribes were writing. In those days Wor Jackie was on the pitch and as much a hero to La Frenais as to thousands of other youngsters. Ian was dead proud of the day he was standing in the paddock and the ball was hoofed out of play straight into his arms.

"I stood there clasping the ball to my chest with my mouth wide open as Jackie ran off the pitch towards me. He obviously wanted a quick throw-in but I was too bemused to do anything but gape. 'Here, give me the ruddy ball,' he yelled. I couldn't believe it. I went back to school on the Monday and told everyone that Jackie Milburn had actually spoken to me."

After his success with the Chelsea film show, La Frenais organised a special night out for the players' wives to see Michael Crawford star in one of his shows before the 1974 FA Cup final, as well as arranging the after-Wembley party.

Of course once Hollywood beckoned and Le Frenais went off to live in Los Angeles, all the fun of regular nights out were vastly curtailed but love (of the Mags) knows no geographical boundaries and it still burns within him today.

We used to travel all over the place in Ian's Roller and actually got a pull once on the A1. The cops couldn't believe that a couple of scruffs with long hair wearing jeans could actually have a right to be driving round in such a gleaming machine. They thought we might have nicked it.

A right couple of likely lads we were!

XXXXX

IT WAS a pleasant enough breaking of bread with

Jack Charlton, manager of Newcastle United for a single season. We had a drop of vino and some decent grub then Big Jack drove me up to Benwell, United's training ground at the time. There was an afternoon session going on and we drifted over to stand and watch.

The ball was being pumped into a crowded penalty area where United's centre-halves were supposed to clear under pressure. Time and again a weak header would fall short just outside the box where a lurking midfielder could have a lash at goal.

Jack, a World Cup winning central defender, was getting more and more angry. Eventually he yelled, "no, no, no," threw down his cap and strode onto the pitch.

Wearing brogues and still with a cigar clenched between his teeth, Charlton demanded the ball be crossed into the box again. When it was he rose like a bird, elbows clearing out anyone who dared to venture onto his toes, and a thumping header sent the ball flying upfield.

Jack took the cigar out of his mouth, turned on his heel, and growled: "That's the bloody way to defend!"

Day I conned my boyhood hero Wor Jackie

OFTEN there can be a real reluctance to throw something away. Sentiment grips and the dustbin remains empty.

So when I delved into my souvenirs tossed into the top of a cupboard, sure enough, there it was.

A Christmas card from 1981. I read the inscription again: "Words cannot express our thanks for getting Jack to the studio. Ten out of 10 and an Oscar!!! Thank you – you looked great on the TV." It was signed Laura and Jackie Milburn.

Ah, the memories. Wor Jackie, my childhood hero. A gentle character with unlimited dignity, master craftsman, a source of hope, an entertainer and, above all, a man with the common touch.

He was a swashbuckling centre-forward in the days of Brylcreemed hair and baggy shorts when soccer grounds were full to bursting and his magical goals were the lifeblood of Newcastle United.

The thank you was a consequence of what in hindsight was an amazing string of events which culminated in a unique showing of *This Is Your Life*, shipped from its London home to Newcastle lock, stock and smoking barrel just so the target (Wor Jackie) could be snared.

It had all began when I was co-author of Jackie Milburn's *United Scrapbook* with the great man himself. A copy of the book found its way onto the desk of Brian Klein, a researcher for the programme at Thames Television. His job was to unearth suitable subjects for *This Is Your Life* and, with Jackie thrust back in the limelight through the publication of a new book, he looked an ideal candidate.

So I got a call from Mr K. He said Jackie Milburn was under consideration for the show and would I co-operate? What followed was three months of meticulous work in total secrecy as the show was put together. Honestly, it was like being an undercover spy.

I had two key roles to play: it was to be my job to approach Laura for her permission and then keep Jackie busy on the actual day of the programme so he hadn't a clue what was happening. Both were vital – if Laura said no there wasn't a show and if Jackie discovered the plot even at the 11th hour before Eamonn Andrews appeared with the big red book, the plug would be pulled. No pressure there, then.

Luckily Laura gave her agreement when I at last got her alone, albeit a little reluctantly knowing Jackie's obsession with privacy. The condition was that the show was filmed up here. No way could she get her hubby on a train to London under the pretext of traipsing round the shops.

The next tricky bit was to keep Milburn busy on the actual

day while his family and guests sneaked off to Tyne Tees Television for rehearsals. Laura told Jack she was going Christmas shopping with her two sisters which left him at a loose end.

A spoof programme entitled *A Chance To Score* had been set up. Jackie – and the audience for that matter – believed he was to be interviewed about our new book. The bait was set.

I believe the tickets for The Show That Never Was have become a bit of a collector's item over the years.

I decided to enlist the help of United's then manager Arthur Cox in my bid to keep Wor Jackie occupied. We spent a couple of hours in Arthur's office chatting about everything from the prog that night to United's hopes and dreams (not my nightmares about Jack taking to his toes).

When finally delivered Milburn walked out through the audience to warm applause. Suddenly the red curtains swished back and there was the Irish leprechaun Eamonn Andrews, beaming that smile which said 'gotcha.' Jackie almost collapsed with shock.

The next half hour was pure nostalgia. Apart from his family and personal friends, a host of celebrities walked on... Bobby and Jack Charlton, naturally, his old England captain Billy Wright, Tom Finney and Raich Carter, as well as Man City goalkeeper Bert Trautmann, who had conceded that Jackie goal after 45 seconds of the 1955 FA Cup final and who had flown in specially from Pakistan.

To top it all Jackie's aunt Bella had journeyed from New York, the first time they had met in 31 years.

Afterwards Jack gave me a big hug. "If I'd known, I would

never have done it," he told me, "but I'm glad it worked. It's been a magical night."

XXXXX

WOR Jackie may have been a fine, fleet footed footballer and a Powderhall sprinter who survived running in the depths of a Scottish winter on New Year's Day.

However he was also a dedicated smoker who always had a packet of fags in his top jacket pocket. He even smoked in the Wembley dressing-room at half-time in the three FA Cup finals, all won gloriously by Newcastle with Milburn the executioner scoring three goals.

There was, however, a price to pay. Jackie, bless him, died of lung cancer aged only 64 on October 9 of 1988.

We all knew long before the end what was inevitable. Jackie gave up his treasured golf days and didn't take up his usual seat amongst us in the Press box at St James' Park, retiring from the *News of the World*.

I had the unenviable task of writing an obituary in readiness for our tribute.

However when the end came I was on a short holiday in Portugal. A glimpse of an English newspaper read over the shoulder of a fellow tourist at the next table revealed the headline: 'A soccer legend dies.' I knew it could only be Wor Jackie.

The rest of my short break was clouded and I flew home on the evening after Jackie's funeral, something which grieved me even more because I so wanted to be present to say goodbye to a friend.

Tyneside was stunned. More than 30,000 lined the streets from his home in Bothal Terrace, Ashington to the cathedral in the centre of Newcastle. Heads bowed, eyes wet, the Geordies paid their homage and the national news on both major TV channels beamed the emotional pictures. The cathedral was packed to the rafters with hundreds standing bare headed in respect outside.

Jackie's ashes were scattered over the Gallowgate End of St James' Park and a new stand was officially named after him.

Laura, as ever, thought of others in her grief and, knowing how unhappy I'd have been at missing Jackie's funeral, she asked me if I would like to give a tribute at a special memorial service which was to be held at the Church of the Holy Sepulchre in Ashington itself.

We all congregated in Laura's house... Laura proudly wearing one of Jackie's Cup medals, daughter Betty, son Jackie and the rest of the family, dear old Cissie Charlton, and Geordie Luke who used to play outside-left for Newcastle. What I said from the pulpit wasn't written but merely delivered from the heart in something of a blur.

Was it good enough? Well, Cissie squeezed my hand as I returned to my seat in the pew next to her. "Aye, Wor Jack would have liked that."

Nothing else really mattered.

Why I was blamed for pin-up boy being cut down to size

THERE are times when bursting pride can instantly change into stomach-churning fear. It did for me on August 7, 1995.

I was chairman of Gateshead and we were playing Newcastle United in a pre-season friendly.

This was a game between the two clubs I loved yet it was much, much more than that. More even than a fundraiser, though for a Conference club money (or the lack of it) is always prominent in the mind.

Sir John Hall was my main sponsor and he just happened to own United so, with the considerable help of manager Kevin Keegan, I was hosting a real glamour match.

Keegan's Entertainers were in full flow by '95 of course and when he announced that he was sending his full first team over the water there was a stampede of United fans down to the International Stadium for tickets.

In the previous couple of months United had caused a sensation by splashing £6m for super striker Les Ferdinand

and a further £2.5m (a snip) on French glamour boy David Ginola.

As Newcastle were playing all their other pre-season friendlies on faraway soil this would be the debuts of Ferdinand and Ginola on Tyneside. Hardly surprisingly, the match was sold out at a capacity 11,750 well before the actual day. That figure is still, of course, Gateshead's record attendance.

If United had 11,000 supporters and Gateshead 750 it mattered not a jot. Nor if we lost 6-0 as we did actually. I had said on radio we would do a lap of honour if we won a corner!

I took my seat proudly in the directors' box to witness the occasion, United's star-packed team giving us a helping hand.

Of course this was a friendly and I reminded our manager to emphasise the point to the lads just before kick-off. Nothing silly please.

However after just a quarter of an hour Mark Hine, our midfielder who loved a tackle, went in hard on Ginola. In a flurry of long hair and forward rolls the Frenchman hit the ground to spark off a charge by United's physio staff.

The Newcastle party in the directors' box turned as one to glare at me. Oh dear, oh dear.

I could see it now. Ginola sidelined before he had even played at St James' Park.

I was out of my seat like a flash and down to our dug-out for an urgent word with the manager. Get the message onto the field, no wild tackles. This isn't a cup tie, it's Premier League players doing us a favour by helping to raise money to pay our wages for the rest of the season. What we were doing by nearly killing Ginola was biting the hand that was feeding us.

Luckily the message got over and the rest of the game was played as it should be.

All's well that ends well but if I close my eyes I can still see Hine launching himself at the highly valued legs of Ginola.

XXXXX

YOU treasure the grand times in football because there are plenty of kicks where the sun doesn't shine.

For me just about the best in over a decade with Gateshead was beating Paul Bracewell's Halifax Town in the first round of the FA Cup on their own midden.

Halifax were a Football League club at the time – November, 2000 – so for a team of part-timers in the Unibond League to deservedly knock them out at their place 2-0 was quite an achievement.

And – sorry Brace – to do it against a former Newcastle star I had regularly worked with here in the North East only heightened my enjoyment, as did a sneaking feeling of revenge.

The Gateshead Post carried an interview with me under a banner headline stating: "It doesn't get any better!"

Halifax were upgrading The Shay at the time so a lot of building work was going on but what really upset us is that at the interval – we were leading 1-0 – the Gateshead players were locked out of their dressing room and were forced to sit in the weights room.

I don't know if it was deliberate or an accident but I do know it fired us up.

Naturally I celebrated somewhat both on the team coach returning to Tyneside and when we got there.

I always remember bursting into this restaurant with various Gateshead folk and being a tad loud.

Suddenly I glanced up and there at a table a few feet away were half a dozen United supporters in their black and white shirts.

I had missed the derby match at St James' Park that day because of the importance of Gateshead's cup tie but knew the Toon had lost 2-1 – it was the game when Thomas Sorensen saved an Alan Shearer penalty.

Immediately I felt guilty about loudly celebrating and went over to say sorry to the Toon Army members.

"No sweat, Gibbo," they said. "Gateshead's result was the only bit of good news we've had."

Bracewell, remember, was viewed by many as more of a Mackem than a Magpie having played for them on three separate occasions AND been their assistant manager.

xxxxx

MARTIN O'NEILL finally made his way to the North East as manager of Sunderland, the club he supposedly supported as a kid back on the Emerald Isle.

My encounter with O'Neill was much earlier when he was a young manager fashioning his considerable reputation at Wycombe Wanderers.

I was chairman of Gateshead – Geordie black and whites

– and we were drawn at Wycombe when on the verge of a Wembley appearance in the FA Trophy final.

Wycombe were the non-league team of the year, destined to win promotion to the Football League and the Trophy in a glorious double under a bright young jack-in-the-box manager.

Yet we almost tucked them up – Paul Dobson, our centre-forward who was the Conference top scorer for two successive seasons, looked a stonewall certainty to score at 0-0 with 92 minutes on the clock but the ball stood up off a divot and he drove wide.

Down t'other end with but seconds remaining Steve Guppy, who later signed for Newcastle, struck a shot which deflected off the heel of one of our defenders and past Simon Smith, who later became Sir Bobby Robson's goalkeeping coach at SJP.

O'Neill ran arms outstretched into the centre circle where he did a somersault in celebration. Honestly I would have throttled him had he been anywhere near me.

As we sat dejectedly in the Gateshead coach waiting for the last stragglers to limp on, O'Neill bounded up the steps.

"Well played lads," he gushed with what I perceived as insincerity.

I looked up. "Do us a favour," I said. "P*** right off."

XXXXX

I AM proud to have signed two FA Cup final goalkeepers at Gateshead.

I took Steve Harper on loan from Newcastle when Kevin

Keegan scrapped the reserve side, leaving young players without any matchday experience.

I did the deal with Steve at Washington Services – we used to pick him up at Easington when he would jump aboard the team coach with his Elvis Presley tapes!

Harps served United for 20 years and richly deserved the startling crowd of 50,793 that turned up for his testimonial at St James' Park in 2013. The other top keeper was Steve Sherwood, who I got on a permanent deal. Harps played for Newcastle in the 1999 cup final against Manchester United while Sherwood was between the sticks when Watford lost to Everton at Wembley in 1984.

It was a final remembered in the main for two things – Watford chairman Elton John crying in the Royal Box and Andy Gray scoring when he headed the ball out of Sherwood's hands.

The Watford team, by the way, included Mo Johnston and two who later played for United: George Reilly and John Barnes, whose great years were spent at Liverpool of course.

When Shack and I got the key to Las Vegas

LEN SHACKLETON was a footballing genius. No question about that. He was known as the Clown Prince of Soccer, a player with twinkling feet and an equally roguish sense of fun.

He was the man who launched a thousand quips. When Shack penned his autobiography he cheekily headlined one chapter 'The Average Director's Knowledge Of Football' and left the page blank.

Shack, ever flamboyant, delivered the perfect introduction when he signed for Newcastle United. In his very first game he scored an unbelievable double hat-trick – yes, six goals – against Newport County who were slaughtered 13-0, still the Magpies biggest victory in their history. Nobody ever topped Shack.

I became a good, good friend of his. We knocked about on United's Fairs Cup excursions across Europe and flew out to Las Vegas together on a North Eastern Sporting Club trip just before the Mags' continental success of '69. Alderman

William McKeag was with us, an aristocratic character who was chairman of United and regularly rowed in public with Stan Seymour, a down to earth working class bloke who called a spade a ruddy shovel.

McKeag spoke like Churchill, wore pinstriped suits, and even occasionally pince-nez glasses (a sort of double monocle) on a cord.

Anyway for weeks before we left for Vegas, McKeag's office were in touch with City Hall officials in the Nevada Desert, pointing out that an influential figure was about to hit town... a former member of the British Parliament, one-time Lord Mayor of Newcastle and chairman of a most influential football club.

Consequently shortly after we arrived, a message winged its way to our hotel. McKeag was to be awarded the Freedom of the City of Las Vegas with a symbolic silver key the official gift of recognition. Obviously the propaganda had worked.

Of course it's no good being honoured if no one knows about it so, as the local hack back home, I was invited to join McKeag on his trip downtown along with Shack, a footballer he had doted upon.

Ten o'clock the following morning a big limousine drew up at the hotel complete with six police motorcycle outriders – all very grand – and we winged our way down the strip to City Hall where we were met with due ceremony.

The Mayor, a guy who looked vaguely like Giant Haystacks, undertook a terrific spiel about what an honour it was to host Mr William McKeag and finished by producing the key to the city with a great flourish. Naturally our Newcastle ambassador replied with great Churchillian delivery and at some considerable length. I swear a couple of the gun-toting Vegas cops nodded off at one time.

When he had finished the Mayor turned to Shack and myself.

"Hi, guys," he boomed. "Here's a key each for you. Have a good day now!" So Leonard Francis Shackleton and John Gibson were awarded the Freedom of the City of Las Vegas along with William McKeag. Not that I reported the fact in the *Chron* when we got back!

Shack was a class entertainment act throughout our stay in the gambling capital of the world.

A footballer renowned for his ball control, he nudged me one night as we walked into the hotel bar.

"Say nowt," whispered Len. "Just keep talking to me."

With that he put his hand in his trouser pocket, pulled out a coin, and flicked it into the air. Without looking he caught the falling coin on the instep of his foot, flicked it up again, leaned forward, and the coin dropped into the top pocket of his jacket. I could see one or two punters staring in disbelief before nudging their mates.

Shack did it twice more before the bar was in uproar. The Yanks nicknamed him 'Yorkshire' because of where he came from and we never paid for another drink in the joint for the rest of our trip.

Shack famously signed for Sunderland after leaving Newcastle of course and he had undertaken a close season trip to America when, because he was an entertainer supreme, he was paid appearance money each game by Sunderland's hosts.

Shack had opened a bank account on t'other side of the Atlantic and never touched the money... until now. He used to knock on my door at night dressed like the star he was in a monogrammed shirt bearing the initials LFS and off we would go to see the shows on the strip, bolstered by his considerable financial backing.

We saw Sammy Davis Jnr, the most professional of artists, and Judy Garland, the most befuddled. Judy, bless her, was no longer walking down the yellow brick road but was suffering greatly from the effects of bodily abuse. The Yanks, however, would forgive her everything and she received a standing ovation just for remembering to face the front when she sang.

Though a joker, Len had great pride in his ability on a football field.

When he was due to play in Jackie Milburn's much delayed testimonial match at St James' Park, Shack secretly trained for a week to get into some sort of shape with the likes of Puskas also gracing Geordie turf.

I vividly recall Shack taking a pass and clipping the ball with the outside of a boot. He dropped on one knee, cocking a finger in its direction, and the ball slowly spun round and returned to him. Not many can do that – but then not many could have executed his coin trick in Vegas either!

XXXXX

UNITED'S former chief executive Freddie Fletcher sadly died not that long ago.

Known as 'the Rottweiler' because of his tough business

acumen, he didn't suffer fools gladly but was nevertheless a Jock with a warm heart and terrific sense of humour.

Freddie was instrumental in building the Entertainers as Sir John Hall's right-hand man. Indeed it was Fletch who came up with the ambitious, nay outrageous, idea of pulling Kevin Keegan from eight years of exile playing golf in Spain to become Newcastle manager.

That it came off was unexpected. That it was such an outstanding success sensational.

I was very much part of the Magpie Group that led the Newcastle revolution in the early nineties and loved the fact that KK was secretly spirited away to Sir John's ancestral pad, Wynyard Hall, overnight before being unveiled the following morning as the saviour of SJP.

Freddie Fletch also stayed and had just clambered into bed at 1.30am when Kevin knocked on his bedroom door. It was pitch dark and being in a strange bedroom, Freddie couldn't find the light switch.

He staggered to the door in his underpants, opened it, and fell headlong down the stairs. Keegan was in stitches.

It turned out that Kev's wife Jean was on the phone panicking because someone was knocking on the door – they lived in an isolated house and she thought that somehow the story of United appointing KK had leaked out and it was the national Press wanting an interview. In fact it turned out to be a guy who had a puncture.

I had alerted the *Chron* as to what was going to happen – Ossie Ardiles sacked over breakfast and Keegan unveiled half an hour later – and we had our front page story all ready before the gun was fired.

I stopped Magpie star walking out on Wembley

THERE is nought more crippling for a footballer, adrenaline pumping, than to be dropped for a big showpiece game.

It's as though someone has suddenly whipped the carpet from under their feet. Their world comes crashing down upon them.

So it was in 1974 with the FA Cup final beneath the twin towers of Wembley fast coming up on the horizon.

United were playing Liverpool, those strutting aristocrats who boasted the likes of Kevin Keegan, John Toshack, Steve Heighway and Emlyn Hughes within their armoury.

Joe Harvey was responsible for team selection and he pulled Stewart Barrowclough to one side to tell him that he would play no part in United's biggest Wembley date since 1955.

Not only was Barrowclough to be banished from the team but there wasn't even to be the consolation of being named the one substitute allowed at that time.

Harvey was gambling. He had decided to sacrifice Barra's raiding down the right wing and instead go with Jinky Smith.

It meant a significant change in style. Where Barrowclough was lightning quick and direct, giving Newcastle width in a middle four, Jinky was more static, would inevitably drift inside to his normal territory, and was all about flicks and nutmegs.

The No.12 shirt was to be worn by Tommy Gibb, another middle four player who had starred in United's European Fairs Cup winning side.

Naturally Stewart was devastated. He would be suited and booted on Saturday when he expected to be stripped and charging down the right touchline.

Barrowclough left Joe, tears in his eyes, and headed straight for his hotel room.

I was tipped off very quickly about Harvey's team selection and, knowing Barra ever so well, decided I must go and see him.

When he opened the door his suitcase was already half full on the bed. He was packing. I knew what that meant. The emotion, the hurt, was all too much and Barrowclough was leaving United's party and heading home.

That would have been a disaster, thrusting his future into grave doubt and creating the wrong impression of a temperamental star who could let a manager down.

We talked for quite a while and eventually, reluctantly, Barra agreed to stay. He saw the sense through his acute hurt.

I had of course talked myself out of a sensational story – United star walks out on Wembley. However some things are bigger than today's headline which tomorrow will inevitably be fish and chip paper.

A knee-jerk reaction could have seen Barrowclough pay a heavy price for the rest of his footballing career and he didn't deserve that.

He was a smashing lad, full of fun, and with not an ounce of malice in his body.

Barra used to come out with a bunch of us night-clubbing. With his gesticulating and horsing around, many was the time a member of the public phoned the manager the next day to say one of his stars had been drunk the night before.

Except that Barra didn't drink. What was perceived as having a Bacardi and coke in his hand was in fact a straight Pepsi.

Jinky was as different a player as was possible. The fans loved him because he was full of tricks. Nutmegging an opponent would bring a chorus of "oles!"

Jinky wasn't a publicity seeker but I managed to get an interview with him during the week of Wembley when he admitted that, be it a cup final or a kickabout in the park, he never had any idea how he would play.

That was some public statement with soccer's showpiece gripping a nation.

United never got a kick at Wembley of course losing 3-0. Malcolm Macdonald, who had scored in every round and away from home, was isolated and cut a lonely figure.

Though SuperMac loved Harvey, he has told me many times since that it was a mistake not a play Barra.

"When Stewie was out there with me I knew exactly what he would do. He would skin the full-back and whip the ball across goal with real pace on it. I would head for the near post, get in front of any marker, and finish."

I must be honest and say I doubt if Barrowlough's presence would have significantly changed anything, Liverpool were that dominant. However it was a major decision to axe him and it could have resulted in the disaster of a headline hugging walk-out.

XXXXX

THROUGHOUT dinner and the speeches thereafter he sat with his cap jammed upon his head.

Not the polite way, some would say, to break bread in such glittering surrounds under the chandeliers of the Newcastle Civic Centre.

However, pop stars can be a law unto themselves and this was one of the grandest around.

Elton John was guest speaker at a Sports Aid Foundation fundraiser and I was sitting next to him as compere for the evening.

Elton had swapped the seating plan around so he had someone he knew by his side rather than a local dignitary three decades or more older than him.

We had spent considerable time in his room at the Gosforth Park Hotel earlier in the day when as chairman of Watford he talked freely on the record about his manager Graham Taylor and players. The *Chron* carried the interview under the banner "John Meets John."

Elton has always had trouble with thinning hair and has gone through many phases, including a transplant. Here the answer was to jam a jaunty cap over his barnet, leaving just the long strands at the back and sides to peek through.

Never one to be over-sensitive about 'film star' looks, he played a game with the audience throughout the evening, repeatedly lifting the cap just a tad as though about to reveal all.

I found the guy terrific company and Eric Steele, a Geordie who began his playing career with Newcastle, kept goal for Elton's Watford side and confirmed that the guy was a diamond.

xxxxx

IT SHOULD have been Snatch Of The Day... Joe Harvey was always recognised as having a canny eye for a player so, even when he was finished in the mid seventies, he still went scouting for the club he loved.

Joe, full of enthusiasm, begged his successor Gordon Lee to buy this young central defender at Partick Thistle.

"Naw," replied Lee brusquely, "I don't like Scottish League players."

The kid's name? Alan Hansen.

On another United excursion into their most favoured hunting ground Scotland to watch what used to be called a tanner ball player, one of the scouting party turned to the other and said: "Oh, I don't know about signing him. He's too small, perhaps we should come back for another look."

"Why?" barked his mate. "He won't have bloody grown any taller!"

The game that never was

UNITED have performed many times in Europe since the Fairs Cup sent Geordies on their merry way.

However, this was the Match That Never Was. A phantom game that never happened but secretly did.

Let me try and explain. Posters all over the holiday resort of Benidorm proclaimed that Newcastle United were to play the local team on a Wednesday at the height of the summer season back in the seventies.

Cars with loudspeakers blaring drove up and down the main streets advertising the game and drumming up support amongst the Brit holidaymakers. It was quite a coup having a top English First Division side taking on a little Spanish league two team and the bars were buzzing. Honestly, it was dafter than a bewigged Tim Healy in Benidorm!

Of course United weren't about to play an official game in the close season so how on earth did the idea get round?

Well, er, it was all down to a drunken bunch of young Geordies on their hols running off at the mouth. Except that these young Geordies were a bit different... they played for United.

Paul Cannell, Alan Kennedy, Derek Craig, Davey Crosson and Billy Coulson were on their jollies and giving it large after having a kickaround with their hotel bartenders and waiters on a nearby piece of wasteland.

One of Cannell's mates let it be known to an admiring Spanish bystander that these lads were tasty because they actually played pro football for Newcastle United.

Oooh, came the delighted reply, would you like another game next Wednesday? Of course they would.

Next thing our intrepid band of funsters knew the posters were out and so were the cars with their loudspeakers. Benidorm v Newcastle was on.

Panic set in but not because the match appeared official. Because United's finest couldn't raise a full team.

The scouts went out round the bars and clubs and a few more footie holidaymakers were roped in...West Ham keeper Mervyn Day, Liverpool striker Phil Boersma, Ray Graydon of Burnley and two Germans from a minor Bundesliga club.

A crowd of around 2,200 turned up expecting the real thing and were rewarded with a 0-0 draw.

All might have been forgotten but the region's English newspaper, the *Costa Blanca News*, actually carried a match report under the headline: "Newcastle held to a goalless draw by Benidorm." And thereby lies another tale.

When Cannell, Kennedy et al arrived home and reported back for pre-season training United's new manager Gordon

Lee wanted to know how his 'new team' had played in Benidorm.

The Guilty Ones tried to blag it but it soon became obvious that Lee knew too much. How?

Well a Geordie fan happened to be on holiday in Benidorm at the same time and contacted me with a copy of the *Costa Blanca News*. On a slow news day in the summer it was like manna from heaven and I gleefully reported the bit of fun in the *Chron* – while the offenders were still in Spain.

I reckoned that if I didn't do it some other paper would when they found it. After all it was now a matter of record in Spain.

Cannell, who like the others didn't hold a grudge, told me later that Joe Harvey popped into the club and casually mentioned his holiday with the missus in Benidorm.

"We were walking along the front when a car went by with a loudhailer claiming Newcastle United were playing Benidorm," said Joe. "The missus asked if we should go. Naw, I said laughing. I knew it would be you, Cannell, on your drunken hols with yer mates!"

xxxxx

TIMES have changed have they not? Especially in football where the one-time paupers are now princes.

When Jackie Milburn led the glorious treble FA Cup winners of the fifties he and his mates were very much paupers despite their successes.

They were paid washers, lived in a modest club house, and travelled into training on the local bus. That's a life as far removed from Wayne Rooney and Gareth Bale as it's possible to get.

I always remember Wor Jackie telling me a tale about when United's skint stars thought they had hit the jackpot.

After one of their Wembley victories a celebration dance was to be held at the Oxford Galleries in the centre of town and rumour had it that the handbags which were to be presented to all the players' wives were to be stuffed with money. Well, the club had made a fortune hadn't it?

Boy were Jackie, Bobby Mitchell and the rest looking forward to the quickstep!

They tried to stifle their delight as one by one the girls trooped up to the bandstand. The handbags were bulging to obscene proportions and in fact the strap of Mrs George Hannah's bag snapped as she carried it back to her table. A dozen pair of eyes registered the same thought: "It's the weight. Whoopee!"

I'll let Wor Jackie take up the tale. "We all remarked as casually as we could how beautiful the bags were then, hardly able to contain ourselves, grabbed them and ripped them open.

"Each one was stuffed with newspaper. Not a sign of the green crinkly stuff.

"We must have looked quite a sight sitting up to our knees in crumpled newspaper but I don't remember being particularly amused at the time.

"To make matters worse we later learned that the club had bought a job lot of 30 bags for seventeen quid!"

Such was their meagre pickings that before the 1951 FA Cup final, their first, the players brought out a brochure "to make a bit of extra jam" and put up trestles in the car park outside the ground to sell them at two bob each.

"Imagine it," Milburn told me, "top First Division stars trying to flog souvenirs to the crowd before dashing off at half past two to get changed. We didn't sell half as many as we should because we would stand nattering to a fan instead of moving him on and getting the next customer."

xxxxx

BOB PAISLEY looked like your favourite uncle, all round faced with slicked back hair, comfy cardigan, and homely voice.

However, the same guy was then the most successful club manager in the history of football.

Uncle Bob from Hetton-le-Hole won a mind-boggling 20 trophies in nine years on behalf of Liverpool as the successor to the flamboyant Bill Shankly.

His haul was bigger than that scooped by the Great Train Robbers – three European Cups, one UEFA Cup, one UEFA Super Cup, six League Championships, three League Cups, and six Charity Shields.

At the time (as now) Newcastle United were winning nowt so it was decided that I should try and discover the secrets of success by going down to see Paisley, a man of our soil, on Merseyside.

Bob agreed and I spent three fascinating days with him in the famous Anfield bootroom and manager's office.

It was also a great opportunity to meet up again with old pals – Terry McDermott, Graeme Souness who I had got to know at Middlesbrough, and Geordies Ray Kennedy and David Hodgson.

Paisley imparted many words of wisdom which included the following bit of advice, probably of particular interest to Newcastle who were always erratic in the transfer market: "The signing of players is absolutely crucial – you must buy well both in terms of ability and character."

"However none of us can be right all the time. The secret is that when you're proved wrong get rid as quickly as you possibly can. Fans then forget about the guy even being here. That's what we do.

"The trouble is a lot of managers try to justify their signings by playing them again and again in the hope they will miraculously improve. Nine times out of 10 they don't."

He was no fool was Bob. An iron fist beneath the velvet glove.

The railwayman who discovered Shearer

JACK HIXON was the most famous and influential scout since Baden Powell. A true Geordie who worked as a clerk for British Rail at the Central Station, he was responsible for discovering young footballers on the playing fields of the North East who would become worth millions upon millions of pounds.

Yet despite being a diehard Newcastle fan until the end he found them all for other clubs, spiriting them away to distant parts.

Hixon's haul was mountainous including as it did Alan Shearer, Ralph Coates, Dave Thomas, Michael Bridges, Brian O'Neil, Trevor Steven, Steve Davis, future managers Mick Buxton and Dave Merrington, and the Ternents Stan and Ray amongst a long list of 47 who made the Football League grade.

He pinched Shearer from under the noses of United, spiriting him off to a far less fashionable club Southampton, and it later cost the Mags a world record £15m to bring him back to where he belonged and should never have left.

Jack was top of the beanstalk, a man who found diamonds in a minefield – yet he almost didn't become a football scout because it would interfere with him supporting United from the terraces of St James' Park.

The opportunity arose when he served on the same Royal Navy ship as Billy Elliott, the one-time Sunderland and England winger. They became pals – Hixon was best man at Elliott's wedding – and Billy managed to persuade Jack to give up his terrace support of Newcastle and scout for Burnley. What the Geordie produced for a small Lancashire mill town club was truly astronomical.

He packed the place with fellow Geordies and the club flourished against the big traditional powers of English football. Around eight or nine Hixon discoveries played together in the First Division and in 1963 Burnley, top of the Central League, sent 11 North East born players to Newcastle for a reserve match. That signed programme was one of Jack's treasured possessions.

Jack became a dear, dear friend and we talked long into many a night, United never far away from the hub of discussion. Hixon's homework was meticulous. He kept a record of every one of his players' birthdays and dispatched a card to drop on the mat come the big day. Part of every tiny personal detail he kept on all his boys, great or small.

Hixon would never admit to his favourite player, nor most talented, but there is no question that Shearer held a special place in his heart. Therefore when England's skipper signed for Newcastle Jack was made up. It became Geordies together again, this time at their ancestral home when, desperately late in his life, Alan arranged for Jack to scout on behalf of the black and whites.

Jack had a cherished dream – he wished for Shearer and Bridges to be united in England garb as the national team's twin strikers. It could have happened, too, but for a bad career-threatening injury to Michael at Leeds when he was soaring towards his pomp.

Instead there was but a brief cameo appearance together at Newcastle. Bobby Robson signed Bridges on loan in 2004 and he went on as a sub for the last 13 minutes of the UEFA Cup semi-final first leg against Marseille at St James' Park. That's as good as it got, though Bridges almost broke the deadlock with a shot that skimmed the post of Fabien Barthez.

When Jack died aged 88 in December of 2009 three fellow Geordies were privileged to address a packed congregation at his funeral in Cullercoats – Shearer naturally, Lawrie McMenemy for whom Hixon scouted at Southampton, and myself.

I was nervous as never before because I wanted to do such a towering figure justice and, yes, I was reduced to tears before leaving the pulpit. But then, darn it, the hardman that is Shearer got the sniffles when words became almost too much.

Alan was like a son to Jack, United a pilgrimage for them both. Only those born within the shadow of the cathedral on the hill would understand.

Appropriately as Jack's coffin entered St George's Church

Mark Knopfler's *Local Hero* filled the air. Unsung hero, maybe, to the public but most definitely a hero to every player who owed him a deep debt of gratitude.

xxxxx

BRIAN JOHNSON is a true rock 'n' roll super star. As the lead singer of heavy metal band AC/DC, Johnson, resplendent in his famous cloth cap, has endlessly belted out his high voltage vocals that have packed the world's biggest arenas and sold more than 200 million albums.

I knew Brian from the early days when he fronted Geordie and was married to Carol, a top of the range Geordie couple.

Of course when AC/DC came along Brian was catapulted into a different sphere. However, a down to earth guy, he has remained with a Geordie accent as thick as a navvy's sandwich and a true fan of Newcastle United to boot.

I remember doing a chat show at a social club in Heaton donkey years ago. When I came off stage and disappeared behind scenes to have a drink in the committee room there was a knock on the door.

A "yeah" brought a head poking round to look inside. A cap perched on top of a mop of black curly hair was instantly recognizable. It was Brian, who had paid his entrance fee and stood at the back to listen to us talking everything Magpie when he could have been a VIP.

Such is Johnson's passion that he once tried to buy the club (before Sir John Hall did) and was elated to play a cameo role in the 2005 film *Goal!* as a Newcastle fan in a bar in California watching a United game. Come to think of it, that wasn't acting. It was just what he does.

xxxxx

BRAVADO is something which requires careful thought. Delivered in a rash moment, it can come back to haunt you.

So it was with a pal of ours when Malcolm Macdonald was king strutter on the Geordie roost.

SuperMac was going off to play for England and when we were enjoying a quiet drink a short while beforehand this guy decided to impress us all. He grandly announced to his girlfriend that each time SuperMac scored he was going to make love to her.

Now at that precise moment Mal had but one England goal, albeit against world champions West Germany.

The only problem when the pair snuggled up in front of the telly was that it was the Cyprus game at Wembley... and SuperMac smashed the goalscoring record by knocking in FIVE.

We didn't see our boastful mate for a few days after that. I reckon he was booked into a health farm to recover from exhaustion!

Match fixers
in Malta

WE were sitting in our hotel bar on the Mediterranean sunshine island of Malta, just after midday enjoying a cup of coffee. It was a pre-season warm weather break and the Newcastle players were milling around in their tracksuits.

Maltese people adore their football, especially England's top flight, and the inevitable autograph hunters were in great attendance. Polite but persistent.

When this guy came up to me inquiring: "Which one is the Newcastle goalkeeper?" I presumed another request for another signature was on its way.

I pointed out Mike Mahoney and got on with my relaxation.

Mike is a good friend of mine and later I wandered over before I went upstairs to my room.

"I presume that fella wanted an autograph," I said nodding in the direction of a disappearing figure.

"Well, no, actually," replied Mahoney pulling me to

one side. "The bugger only wanted me to chuck in a couple of goals in our match!"

He what? Did I hear right? Someone wanting to fix a match?

Yeah, as it turned out. The Maltese love gambling as much as they love football and some unscrupulous figures, as in lots of places dotted round the world, want to make a killing.

United from England's first division losing to part-timers in Malta would produce lengthy betting odds. Hadn't Newcastle just finished fifth and qualified for the UEFA Cup that upcoming season of 1977-78?

Of course Mahoney was outraged and sent the guy packing. No way was that ever going to happen. Hell would freeze over before Mahoney sold his soul. However because the approach was low key and appeared to come from an individual rather than an organised gang, and as the game was only a friendly, Mahoney decided to take it no further. No need for an official inquiry, no need to open what could be a can of worms.

Still we were shaken. It was hardly a run of the mill thing. At least as far as we knew.

United were playing two friendlies against Sliema Wanderers and Floriana. Sliema were beaten 4-0 at the Empire Stadium in Gzira – Malta still had hard grounds in the seventies – but Floriana managed a 1-1 draw. What if they had won?

As it happened United nicked their best player Raymond Xuereb, who had notched the equaliser to Alan Gowling's opener.

Xuereb was invited over for a trial and played a few reserve games. Though Mr X was never going to make the A list he became a regular in Malta's national team for seasons.

It was on this trip that I met a fanatical fan called Louis Azzopardi who I kept in touch with for years, so much so that I was made president of United's Maltese Supporters Club.

Louis lived five minutes from our hotel in Rabat and I was invited over to meet his wife and daughters.

When the Newcastle party left Malta, Louis was at the airport with his family proudly waving a banner which read "Howay the Lads."

Later he came over to a Newcastle match at St James' Park and met his great hero Jackie Milburn. Football often throws up truly nice friendships.

XXXXX

THERE we were standing in the cool late night air outside our hotel in Sheffield. Some people in pyjamas, me cursing that our beautifully chilled bottle of white wine was obviously getting a tad warm.

We were all the subject of a fire alarm that meant the hotel had to be evacuated for safety reasons.

All very well except that this was literally the eve of the 1974 FA Cup semi-final at Hillsborough and Newcastle United's finest were loitering in the street.

Within a few hours (because the night wasn't young) the Magpies were due to do battle with Burnley for the right to play beneath the twin towers of Wembley. With such a task rapidly looming the players ought to have been confined to their rooms contemplating a good night's sleep while the rest of us downstairs talked excitedly about our aspirations for the following afternoon.

I was doing just that with Ian La Frenais, scriptwriter of the *Likely Lads*, *Porridge*, and *Auf Wiedersehen*, *Pet*, when the alarm meant abandon ship. I mean, were we Geordies jinxed? Was Wembley not meant to be? Was it written in the night sky that we had to stagger from crisis to crisis?

This latest inconvenience was par for the course in a chaotic, maddening build up to the semi-final, seen by many as the most important cup-tie of all because you are so near but yet so far.

What ought to have been straightforward was anything but after an astonishing cup tie that was scrubbed from the record books.

In the end United were forced to play THREE quarter-final ties – they won two of them – two First Division matches, and the semi all in the month of March.

They finished up with four games in 12 days and every one a strength-sapping, tension-filled encounter.

Originally on March 9 Newcastle defeated Nottingham Forest 4-3 in the Cup, having miraculously recovered from 3-1 down and with only 10 men to boot. What ought to have been hailed as the greatest comeback since Lazarus was wiped from the records by the FA upon Forest's appeal because of a pitch invasion by Newcastle fans.

So it was off to a neutral ground Goodison Park to decide all. Except it didn't. The game ended 0-0 after extra time.

Burnley were waiting delightedly in the wings as Newcastle and Forest punched themselves to a standstill.

I recall Burnley's local reporter saying to me after a two-hour slog first time around that Burnley would take an exhausted United apart. I feared he might be right.

The Magpies' build-up to that semi at Hillsborough read: Monday, March 18: 0-0 with Forest at Goodison; Thursday 21: 1-0 victory over Forest on the same ground; Saturday 23: Liverpool 0-0 at home in the First Division; Saturday 30: date of Burnley semi at Hillsborough.

What with such a tiring programme – and a night standing outside their hotel – United ought to have been fodder for a refreshed Burnley.

Instead they triumphed against mountainous odds because of two very super Macs. Malcolm Macdonald and Willie McFaul.

McFaul kept Burnley out and SuperMac knocked them out with two goals which underlined his enormous brute strength and power of pace.

First he carried centre-half Colin Waldron on his back to lash the ball home then finished off a move from Newcastle's penalty area to theirs in the twinkling of an eye.

John Tudor hooked the ball out from a Burnley corner, Terry Hibbitt standing out on the left wing found Malcolm with one caressing touch, and United's No.9 arrowed a low shot into the net. Paddy Howard has since called Hibby's pass the best he ever saw.

The Pyjama Game was won. It was United who had the fire not Burnley despite everything and Wembley lay ahead.

Cloughie to the rescue

BRIAN CLOUGH was a man of utter contradiction, one moment a caring support, the next cruel in his cutting observations.

It was as though he relished doing the unexpected. Certainly Cloughie was never a conformist. What he was, of course, was a managerial genius.

I worked with him at close proximity over many years and we became friends. However never would I pretend to know what made him tick – I doubt if he knew – yet that was the total fascination.

Often I saw both sides of Cloughie. The caring man who lent support to the underdog was never better displayed than when we unexpectedly met pre-season on the holiday isle of Jersey.

Brian was with his wife Barbara, yes not with his club despite the fact we were well into pre-season activity. That was why I was there, covering United's build-up.

When I walked into the hotel restaurant for dinner I took

a table by myself. The players were naturally sitting together along the full length of the back wall.

I hadn't noticed Mr and Mrs C because I wasn't expecting their presence even though Cloughie always did the unexpected.

"Why aren't you sitting with the official party?" inquired Brian in that distinctive nasal drawl.

Trying to explain was futile. He took it as a slight against me, a work colleague of his, and made a great fuss of the waiter moving me onto his table "for the rest of your trip."

United were equally surprised to see Cloughie breaking bread and afterwards when we adjourned to the bar one of the directors made a great show of approaching Brian, handed extended in welcome.

"Excuse me," replied our European Cup winning manager. "I'm speaking with a friend. I'll talk to you later."

With that Cloughie turned on his heel and inquired: "Where were we, John?" The bar was duly impressed.

However there was another side to Cloughie, displayed during visits to Gateshead and Seahouses as part of the many chat shows we did together throughout the North East.

Such was Cloughie's commitment to our public appearances that he motored up from Derby, picked me up in Newcastle, and travelled on to the outpost of Seahouses for one show. Then went back the same night after buying fish and chips to eat en route.

I doubt if many today would pay such lip service to football fans – crikey most wouldn't wish to be put out if they had only to motor the hour from Newcastle.

Clough being Clough, when we arrived at our northerly

seaside resort and got changed in the dressing-room he emerged in a magnificent, sharp silver grey suit... with trainers and no socks!

We had been greeted upon entering the car park by an excited doorman – you don't get many stars like Cloughie appearing in Seahouses I guess!

The gushing was well over the top until Brian barked: "You go and do your job and I'll do mine." The ultimate put down. I was crushed, never mind the guy.

When we appeared at Gateshead it was much the same. Cloughie ignored a reception committee of local dignitaries in his honour, with drinks and nibbles and much fawning, to walk straight from the door onto the stage and refused to come off in the interval, remaining firmly in his seat signing autographs.

In between he suddenly veered off the hot topic of football to launch a stinging attack on the audience for voting Margaret Thatcher into power. This in a Labour stronghold!

Brian was, of course, a one-off as a manager as well but my how successful he was!

He took the likes of Frank Clark, thought by Newcastle United to be washed up, and breathed new life into his ageing career – so much so that Clarkie won the old First Division championship AND the European Cup with Nottingham Forest.

How United could have done with Brian in his pomp – and it might have happened.

I was there when Peter Ratcliffe and John Waugh, two future members of the Magpie Group that eventually propelled Sir John Hall into the St James' Park boardroom, tapped Cloughie about becoming a Mighty Magpie.

And the old centre-forward who brought goals to Sunderland was interested enough to talk long into the evening shadows about the possibility. Pity it never happened.

xxxxx

BUDGIE, it could be said, was a barrel short of a full load.

However that's the way it's supposed to be with top of the range goalkeepers.

John Burridge once told me without a flicker of amusement how he and Arthur Cox – two former Newcastle residents as wacky as one another – concluded transfer negotiations.

Cox wanted Budgie to sign for Derby County and when talks reached an impasse, Arthur said he would make them a cup of tea. He left, locking the door of his manager's office on the way out to make certain Budgie remained his 'prisoner.'

Except that Budgie managed to force open a window, climbed out, and made a dash for his car. He had to drive up the road, turn on the roundabout at the top, and head back down the other side past the Baseball Ground. By then Coxy had emerged red with rage and threw the teapot at him as Budgie roared by!

"I sent Arthur a Christmas card every year as I did with all my old managers but he always returned it ripped up in the same envelope," said a puzzled Budgie.

John, a fitness fanatic, lapped up the adoration that flowed when he performed his never-before-seen somersaults as part of his warm-up routine carried out on the pitch. He sat on the crossbar in one game and wore a Superman outfit under his kit when playing for Wolves. Eccentric? You betya!

Everyone in the game had a Budgie story and United director Peter Mallinger was no exception.

"Whenever we were away from home I could look out of my hotel window early in the morning and there was Budgie working out on his own in the car park," Peter told me. "He would be doing press-ups and stretching exercises before any of the other players were awake."

Even sitting round the hotel lounge was too boring for Budgie. He would collect half a dozen apples and oranges, give them to Mallinger, and tell him to throw one at him when he was least expecting it.

Such were Burridge's reflexes that not once, Mallinger assured me, did he manage to penetrate John's guard and score a direct hit.

xxxxx

MANY was the argument I would have with Gordon Lee over the value of a goalscoring centre-forward.

Lee famously declared that he had no time for superstar players and proved it by getting rid of Malcolm Macdonald at Newcastle and then Duncan McKenzie at Everton.

This day there were only the two of us sitting in his small office in the bowels of St James' Park and once again we got round to talking about SuperMac who Lee knew was a friend of mine.

I argued that Mal's goals – up to 30 a season – made him invaluable and virtually guaranteed any team he played in would never be relegated. Lee, on t'other hand, wanted to make a big deal about Macdonald's work rate and failure on occasions to track back.

I told him SuperMac had taken the advice of local legend Jackie Milburn when he first arrived. Wor Jackie told him to always keep something in the tank to make one of his blistering 25-yard dashes in the 90th minute to win the match. Jackie himself did that on many occasions.

However Lee would have none of it so, exasperated, I said: "What about Jimmy Greaves then?" He was at the time the greatest scoring machine in English football.

"I wouldn't play him," insisted Gordon.

"All right," I replied standing up, "I think I'll be leaving now."

Lawrie Mac to the rescue

AT THEIR lowest ebb United produced a signing that was electrifying, so mind-boggling that it would rock not only Tyneside but have reverberations as far afield as this great game is played.

In was the dawn of the eighties and Newcastle, once revered but now lost in the mediocrity of the Second Division's hinterlands, were going nowhere.

Kevin Keegan on the other hand was a world superstar twice crowned European Footballer of the Year, current England captain, and a European Cup winner with Liverpool.

Yet despite spiralling odds United were ambitious enough, far seeing enough and brave enough to go out and sign him.

KK had been fashioning miracles on the south coast with Southampton but with a get-out clause fixed as low as £100,000 the word was circulating that Keegan was in the marketplace.

Manchester United were linked with him – fair enough –

and then the Mags got a mention. A publicity stunt, sniffed the rest of the country.

Within the *Evening Chronicle* we were buzzing with anticipation. We knew the Keegan interest was genuine but United, anxious not to cause waves at a delicate stage of negotiations, wouldn't stand up the story with quotes. We desperately needed a breakthrough.

Often on these occasions it comes through old contacts, people a newspaperman knows in the game who are willing to give a tip off on the back of friendship and so it was to prove here.

Keegan was already committed to playing for Southampton against Utrecht in Holland and had to fly out to rejoin the club's pre-season tour. The Saints had been guaranteed a fee of £15,000 for the game (not bad in those days) – but only if the England skipper was in their side.

With the match over it was decision day and I was sitting hundreds of miles away across the North Sea without a firm break on the biggest story in quite a while. The front page was cleared in anticipation but nobody was saying a dicky bird and the clock was ticking away ominously.

In desperation I attempted to contact Southampton boss Lawrie McMenemy at his hotel. After much to-ing and fro-ing the nearest I got to Lawrie was John Mortimore, his No.2. It seemed the whole world was chasing the Big Man and John was his buffer.

Mortimore listened sympathetically but explained he couldn't say a word. Those were his instructions. Another idea bites the dust.

I was preparing a speculation piece when the phone rang on my desk 10 minutes before edition time and about an hour after my negative conversation with Mortimore. Damn it, I thought, another interruption.

"Hello."

"John, it's Lawrie McMenemy."

"Who?"

"Lawrie. Listen mate, I haven't got much time. Keegan is flying direct to Newcastle on a British Caladonian flight. His plane will arrive at 10 to 12. Be there. Newcastle are planning a Press conference at the Gosforth Park Hotel tonight."

As Lawrie talked he was constantly interrupted by the 'beep, beep, beep' from the coin box quickly followed by the sound of gilders being fed in to keep us connected. There was no comfort of a mobile phone.

McMenemy was ringing me from Amsterdam Airport before he and the rest of the Southampton party boarded one plane for the south coast and Keegan another for Tyneside.

Lawrie, bless him, knew I was in trouble and pulled me out of a hole.

That's friendship – we had grown up together in footballing terms when I was a cub reporter covering non-league Gateshead many, many moons ago and he was their fresh faced young coach. He had attended my 21st birthday party and we had never lost touch.

As a direct result of McMenemy's call I met the plane, carried an all-editions story including an airport photograph of a chilly Keegan stepping onto Geordie soil, and attended the evening Press conference safe in the knowledge that we had been nailed on every step of the way.

The official signing on August 19, 1982 was described by chairman Stan Seymour Jnr as "an occasion which will stand out in the history of this great club."

So it did. KK won United promotion as a player and returned some time later to manage a side on the brink of the old Third Division and propel them to runners-up in the Premier League, building in the process the Entertainers, one of the finest squads ever to be assembled in our name.

XXXXX

THERE was a touch of Ant and Dec about them. Even Morecambe and Wise when it came to hamming it up.

Kevin Keegan and Terry McDermott may have at first sight seemed an unlikely couple but their partnership progressed from the playing field into the manager's office at St James' Park.

Both were crucial to Arthur Cox's plans to resurrect Newcastle and take them back into top-flight football and the spirit they created went a long way to achieving it.

Cox, with his close cropped hair and military muscle, used to work the players like the SAS so one day Keegan and McDermott turned up in full army kit, crawling through the undergrowth at the training ground. And another time Terry Mac dressed in flowing Arab robes and, head bowed, walked into chairman Stan Seymour's office pretending to make a bid for KK.

For a split second Seymour bought it too!

When I heard about the Arab 'bid' I persuaded McDermott to get into character again just for our cameras. Always full of fun, he didn't need any prompting.

Never a coach, a few folk used to wonder exactly what Terry did when Keegan brought him back upon being appointed manager.

It was rumoured he went for the *Racing Post*, got the lunchtime sarnies, and put out the cones on the training pitch. That was harsh – but funny. What McDermott most certainly did do was to launch his own manhunt whenever a temperamental Keegan walked out, which he did on more than one occasion.

Terry The Peacemaker would go douse him down and return him to the fold. Eventually, of course, KK effected his escape once too often and that was the end of him.

xxxxx

SADLY for me there was a bittersweet ending to Kevin Keegan's days as a player. In effect he tucked me up.

KK publicly came out against a book I had written with his full permission telling his life story. I can't pretend I wasn't deeply wounded and confused.

There seemed no apparent reason for it but I found out much later that, by accident, my book was to hit the shops before the official club brochure marking his sudden retirement and was therefore likely to cream the market with the club unable to fully cash in. They didn't like that.

It was political – I was in the way – but I found it hard to take after the working relationship I had forged fronting

Keegan on a series of official club Scottish and Newcastle Road Shows.

A Press conference was called behind my back to disassociate Keegan from the book despite him agreeing to it at a long meeting we had in his room at the Gosforth Park Hotel, when he furnished me with a number of invaluable contact numbers.

There's no lying down in the face of adversity – United only recognise strength – and in response I went round every radio and TV station the following day defending myself.

If only someone had spoken with me instead of making a public stand behind my back I could have come to some financial arrangement with United.

But to heck with it. KK had been one of the most inspiring players ever to pull on a black and white shirt and when he unexpectedly returned as manager we were able to work together once more as though nought had happened.

That's the way of it sometimes between hack, football club and certain footballers. We can through necessity sing from different hymn sheets!

When United were a riot in Dublin

PERHAPS I've just been unlucky but on the two occasions I've set Geordie foot in the fair city of Dublin on soccer business I've ended up engulfed by a full blown riot.

The first time was with Newcastle United, the second England but no matter. Both resulted in the hurling of much more than obscenities.

United were drawn against Bohemians in the UEFA Cup of 1977-78 which was just a hop, step and jump across the water to the capital of Ireland's Republic.

As the two-legged tie was against part-timers it looked a jolly for Newcastle, even amid a shocking run of poor form on home soil, except that this was the time of the shameful terrorist atrocities on both sides of the divide which were scarring a green and pleasant land.

Still we ventured forth optimistically enough. I had made my usual recce to size up the opposition and perhaps ought to have been warned.

The Bohs officials were wonderful, generous hosts who took me everywhere across a beautiful city and even returned to my hotel in the evening for dinner and drinks. All most cordial until midnight approached and, fuelled by a few Guinnesses, the mood suddenly took on an edge of 'us and them.' Now I was a Brit and they Irish!

Anyway on to match day. The football was tame but not the crowd. The Press box at Dalymount Park was three-quarters of the way down the pitch towards the end where Bohs fans were waving the Tricolour en masse and occasionally bursting into anti-English chants.

Still, I'd seen and heard worse... until a Newcastle fan, sitting immediately behind me, decided to unfurl a Union Jack. Now it had United's name upon it amid the stripes and was not raised intentionally to be provocative but it was a Union Jack nonetheless and the response from the Tricolour was immediate and ferocious.

A hail of half bricks were launched in its direction which meant, when they fell slightly short of their target, they thudded onto the desk where I was sitting. Or rather by now under which I was sheltering.

I squinted out from my bolthole just as my old drinking pal from up the road in Whickham, Mike Mahoney, went down as though shot by a sniper. What had happened was a half brick had bounced off the back of his head!

Afterwards I accused Super Goalie of being chicken. "Jack Charlton," I maintained, "would have headed the brick into the crowd and spat out his teeth."

The Welsh referee immediately took off all the players as the Garda attempted to restore peace. All 11 of them on duty to try and contain a 25,000 crowd. As though they couldn't anticipate trouble!

After a break of quarter of an hour the game restarted, once more uninspiring as it had been, and United drew 0-0 to eventually kick out Bohs 4-0 in the second leg at St James' Park.

I didn't return until 1995 when England played Jack Charlton's Republic of Ireland at Lansdowne Road. This time the game didn't finish.

One-time United striker David Kelly gave the green jerseys the lead on 21 minutes and that sparked off the unrest pre-planned by Combat 18, a neo-Nazi organisation which attached itself to the England national side.

Seats were ripped up and hurled down onto the pitch and, rightly, the so-called friendly was abandoned.

United boss Richard Dinnis, no more than a puppet, survived for a short while after the 'success' against Bohs but was sacked immediately following United's exit in the next round.

Player power had put him in charge after Gordon Lee took to his toes midway through the previous season. Dinnis, his No.2, was actually carried round the SJP pitch shoulder high by those players who were attempting to dictate club policy.

The dressing room had been split into two camps under Lee. There were the likes of Malcolm Macdonald, Terry Hibbitt and Paddy Howard in the anti-Lee divide, Alan Gowling, Geoff Nulty, Mickey Burns and Tommy Craig with Leapy Lee.

They were the boys who powered an innocent of no

experience into the manager's seat. Dinnis had been nought but a coach and in the transfer market he was a rank amateur with no contacts.

Come the new season United won the opener 3-2 at home to Leeds but then proceeded to lose no fewer than 10 First Division matches off the belt, which plummeted them to bottom spot.

During that time they also lost at home to Millwall in the League Cup and were turfed out of the UEFA Cup by Bastia on home ground.

Dinnis had as much chance of survival as a snowflake in the Sahara.

If directors can make mistakes in appointing managers brother did the players here. Bad judgement based on self preservation I'm afraid.

Mind you, the directors fared no better in their choice of a replacement. Bill McGarry, who revelled in a reputation as a guy tough as Robert Mitchum, made Dinnis look like Little Lord Fauntleroy and, sure enough, eventually took the silver bullet himself.

xxxxx

TOMMY CRAIG was a footballing artist whose left foot could create wonderfully bold strokes of vivid colour.

He was the man who took over the mantle of United playmaker from Terry Hibbitt and made dreams come true.

In a distinguished playing career the ginger topped Scot played 157 games for Newcastle, skippering them in the 1976 League Cup final at Wembley, as well as performing honourably in the colours of Aston Villa, Sheffield Wednesday and Aberdeen. When he won his lone Scotland cap while with United it meant he had played for his country at every level of international football, a feat performed only by a chosen few.

Craig moved effortlessly into coaching, which he initially did at Newcastle of course, and became assistant manager at Glasgow Celtic, Hibernian, Aberdeen and Scottish League Cup winners St Mirren. Scotland Under 21s also benefited from his expertise.

That's called experience and indicates a sound footballing brain.

However we all have our Achilles heel. Everyone can make a mistake when it comes to judgement. And, boy, did TC drop an almighty clanger while operating on the left tramline on behalf of the black and whites.

United were drawn against Bastia in the UEFA Cup of 1977-78 after defeating the part-timers of Bohemians. I visited Napoleon's island of Corsica for a good sniff around before the first leg – what a journey that was of changing planes – and then returned in a more convenient way abroad United's charter.

Hardly in a rich vein of form – indeed United were truly awful when on First Division duty – they still managed somehow to remain in the tie losing only 2-1 to the French club.

Afterwards I was chewing the fat with Craig about precisely where that left Newcastle, buoyed by the scoring of an away goal secured through Paul Cannell.

"You know, Gibbo," said TC quizzically, "that was

the worst display I've ever seen from a supposedly world class player."

Quite a statement!

Tommy was referring to Johnny Rep, the Dutch international striker well decorated throughout a career more sparkling than a chandelier.

True, he hadn't torn up any trees against the Mags despite playing at home but was TC (Top Cat after the cartoon character) being just a little premature?

Let us consider Rep's reputation. He had scored Ajax's winning goal against Juventus in the '73 European Cup final and knocked in four goals as a super Dutch side reached the '74 World Cup final.

Months after the Newcastle tie Rep was to lead Holland to back to back World Cup finals, notching en route of course.

Surely Craigy was a bit premature, especially considering United's shocking league form. Sure enough when Bastia arrived at St James' Park for the return Rep was revved up. He tore United apart, scored two stunning goals, and United were destroyed 3-1.

Oh dear, did TC look sheepish as he trudged past me after the match. "Aye, Gibbo, I know" he said. "Keep it shut." Bastia went on to the UEFA Cup final, by the way.

United star who collapsed in street on match days

THERE is nothing like a mystery to stir the blood as well as launch wild theories as to what really happened.

The imagination runs amok as limited pieces of information take on sinister proportions in the minds of theorists.

And football, so beloved by so many, is a ready vehicle for public speculation.

A big club like Newcastle United, followed slavishly by 50,000 and more fanatics, is the perfect breeding ground for public debate in pub and club across the Geordie landscape.

So it was in April of 1968 as United were approaching their finest hour, the winning of a European trophy for the first and only time.

Joe Harvey had gambled to reshape his team, killing the threat of relegation and replacing it with European qualification in only 12 months. To do so Harvey sold his biggest asset in Alan Suddick and used the £60,000 to sign three players: Dave Elliott, John McNamee and Tommy Robson. Elliott, a young man who had honed his skills with Gateshead as a school kid and then Sunderland, was a chunky, driving player with power and presence. Just what Harvey needed at the time.

However there was a problem, a huge problem, and it unexpectedly surfaced one Saturday morning when United were in London to play West Ham.

As usual on the morning of a match the players went out for a stroll to kill time. Elliott disappeared with his room-mate Ollie Burton and skipper Jim Iley while I stayed in the hotel lounge having a coffee with McNamee. Harvey, coach Ron Lewin, and director Fenton Braithwaite were at the next table.

After a while United's manager was paged and told that he was wanted on the phone. He came back looking deathly white to say that Elliott had collapsed in the street and been rushed to hospital.

All hell was let loose as Harvey and Braithwaite dashed off to Charing Cross Hospital and I grabbed a phone to contact my office.

That night Dave's sudden collapse in a London street and the fact that he was detained in hospital was splashed on the front page of the *Chron* and wild stories were being told in every pub on Tyneside.

I've always felt that there is a distinct advantage in hacks travelling overnight with the team and, whenever possible, staying in the same hotel. It can produce devastating results as it did here.

Lurid tales of fighting amongst players circulated for

weeks afterwards with people flatly refusing to accept it was all due to the very personal physical problems of one individual and nought else.

The whisper I heard in due course was that Elliott had taken a fit. The trouble was, of course, that both a confused club and its players remained tight-lipped which only fuelled the speculation. It was, perhaps, understandable in the immediate aftermath given that we're not talking of anything untoward but equally of something which could seriously jeopardise his playing career. Under such circumstances Dave deserved privacy and respect.

However sadly all was not over. The following season with United storming towards European Fairs Cup glory it happened again. And again Ollie was involved.

We were in Glasgow for a huge semi-final first leg match against Rangers. Burton and Elliott decided to take the air when, once more, Dave collapsed on the pavement.

Ollie sprinted back to the team hotel and the club doctor David Salkeld rushed out to look after Dave who was put to bed in the same room as Burton.

When a top footballer dramatically collapses not once but twice in the street of great cities on the day of combat it naturally causes a tidal wave of panic.

Harvey decided he couldn't play Burton in such a massive match, given his state of mind and how he had reacted on the field the last time it happened in London, and that meant a dramatic call up for McNamee.

We now had another story on our hands. McNamee could bend iron bars with his teeth. He had been hounded out of Scotland because of his disciplinary record and here he was going back for a European semi-final. Not only that but he was a former Celt about to face the auld enemy.

Big Mac, never one to remain shyly tight lipped, announced to the Scottish Press that he could play Colin Stein, Rangers illustrious centre-forward, "standing on one leg."

Considering 75,580 packed into Ibrox McNamee could have made a dirty big rod to beat himself with, but instead he was truly magnificent, United earned themselves a 0-0 draw, and one foot was already in Budapest for the final. The whole unfortunate double episode with Elliott was only cleared up several years later when, coming up to Tyneside from his Newport home for a Fairs Cup reunion, Dave sat with me reliving his nightmare.

He had suffered two epileptic fits for the first time in his life but United in their wisdom decided the party line should be that he had fainted. All was swept under a very big carpet.

Naturally it had left Elliott feeling aggrieved, something which has lived with him ever since. Today he would have had the full support of his club. Back then United simply couldn't get him off their books quick enough. He was sold to Southend United.

Elliott still takes tablets to control his epilepsy yet he continued with his football career. Only five times in his life has he suffered from a fit, only once when with Southend.

Football thankfully has moved out of the dark ages since Dave Elliott was abandoned.

XXXXX

BOB STOKOE bled black and white and entered United

legend when he became an FA Cup winner at Wembley in 1955 yet they erected a statue to him down the road on Wearside!

Stokoe was a ferocious competitor and I fell foul of his aggressive bias, blamed for supposedly selling his spiritual home to one of his young players at Carlisle.

That footballer was Peter Beardsley, destined without question in my opinion to become the most gifted performer ever in Newcastle's history. At the time Beardo was fashioning his budding reputation at the soccer outpost of Carlisle having made a late entry into the professional ranks and Stokoe was his club manager.

We ran a competition at the *Chron* to find the North East's Most Promising Newcomer. I was the chairman of the panel of judges with an ice skater and jockey amongst the challengers to Beardsley and Sunderland starlet Rob Hindmarch.

For me there was but one winner and, duly, Peter received his trophy at an awards night held in the restaurant beneath the Odeon Cinema in Newcastle. Naturally I carried an interview with our Most Promising and, as part of his enthusiasm, I quoted Beardsley as saying he would love one day to play for his hometown club Newcastle. Hardly sensational or controversial, I suggest, merely the obvious ambition of a young sportsman still learning his profession.

I thought nothing more of it until the Sunday morning, early doors, when the door bell jarred me into life.

I opened the door and there stood a familiar figure, lean in mackintosh and trilby. Bob Stokoe.

Now I lived in Whickham at the time and he on the west

coast. He knew neither my address nor phone number yet on a Sunday morning when most enjoyed a lie-in he had motored from Carlisle at an ungodly hour in search of me.

Still a bit bemused, I invited Bob in for a chat upon which I was subjected to a tirade accusing me of tapping Peter on behalf of Newcastle. Really? Did Stokoe, bless him, think a talent as precocious as Beardsley's could remain inside the narrow confines of Carlisle United FC?

I couldn't take it too seriously and to lighten the mood asked Bob if he wanted soldiers with his chucky eggs and a cosy on his pot of tea! No laughter.

Eventually Bob simmered down and we talked football as two lovers of the game do. We ended up parting as though friends hoping it wouldn't be too long until we met again.

Beardsley, of course, went off on an educational excursion to Vancouver Whitecaps, Manchester United took him for a look which confirmed potential, and Newcastle signed him TWICE in his illustrious career which was topped by 59 England caps and winning the First Division championship crown on two occasions with Liverpool.

I take no credit for spotting Peter's early promise. If he played on your front lawn with the curtains drawn and you wore dark glasses his light would still come shining through. That's how good he was.

John Hall's bloody war to take over Newcastle United

SIR JOHN HALL fought a bloody two-year battle to boot out Newcastle United's blinkered directors and usher in Kevin Keegan and his Entertainers.

However there was increasingly desperate in-fighting and many fallen victims before victory was claimed.

United are of course big business and people don't give up control easily. More likely they have to be carried screaming to the negotiating table. From day one the *Chronicle* decided to put their weight behind the campaign with a bold logo showing a disgruntled Magpie alongside the words: "After 35 bleak years why are we waiting?"

It was, as Hall was to acknowledge, a particularly brave decision by a local newspaper because success was far from guaranteed.

I was designated to be the *Chron's* voice during the campaign launch as the eighties came to an end which, of course, put me on a direct collision course with those sitting on high as the powerbrokers of St James' Park. Rapidly relations between Hall's Magpie Group and United's board became increasingly fraught. Good manners were abandoned in the heat of battle, dirty tricks abounded, and threats became more wild by the month.

In the end the Magpie Group were buying up shares at a mindblowing £1,000 a time with John Waugh, Peter Ratcliffe and Malcolm Dix criss-crossing the country for clandestine meetings with those possessing paper power.

The breakthrough came when George Dickson, the biggest of shareholders, quit the board and sold out to Hall.

I was used throughout as a go-between, meeting up with certain directors for unofficial talks. It led to some bizarre experiences which would have rested more easily within the pages of a spy novel.

For example at one meeting held in a private house I was taken into the kitchen at a critical point during negotiations and the cold water tap was turned full on so that if I was wired, voices could not be clearly heard.

The obsession with being recorded was always prevalent. I was ordered before one coming together with a current director to take him away from the designated meeting place in case it was bugged and instead find a quiet corner of a hotel lounge not in his territory and not of his choice. Hey, guys, I'm just a poor hack not James Bond. Often shaken but not stirred!

Naturally I became fair game in a brutal war and was warned that once this was all over I would never be allowed into SJP again. Ah, I replied full of bravado if nought else, but what if we win. Will you get back in?

At one stage I was fleetingly given a bodyguard, a former SAS man. Honest, I kid not!

It's ironic, isn't it, that out of bloody conflict should come respect and even friendship. Peter Mallinger was one of the Newcastle board directly in the firing line and consequently he took some heavy hits and of course eventually lost his position of power.

It was inevitable that I would be involved in a one on one with Mallinger when there was no holding back but, battle over, I later came across Peter once again at his new football club. He bought Kettering Town at a time when I was chairman of Gateshead and we met regularly for Conference confrontations. And, yes, we became friends who kept in regular contact.

Friends again, actually, because we had touched base long before war broke out.

Whenever I wrote a book on United this guy from Leicester would get in touch ordering a copy and asking if I would sign it. I was prolific at the time, which meant he had many black and white volumes and we became chatty without ever meeting one another.

The guy was Peter Mallinger, who had lived at Archbold Terrace in Jesmond and paid his first visit to St James' Park as an impressionable 10-year-old. What a visit it turned out to be, too – the Magpies slaughtered Newport County 13-0, still the club's record victory, and new signing Len Shackleton scored six on his debut.

There was no question that Peter was a genuine fan, he merely suffered because the timing of his move onto the board (17 years after he bought my first book) wasn't great. I liked him and he was big enough to rise above political problems.

The one nagging thought throughout a campaign which took two long years to reach its conclusion was what if the change didn't work? What if United were no better off? My intentions may have been honourable as a fan sick of relentless mediocrity but when replacing power you must do so with something better.

Regardless of what was to emerge long term, the rise and rise of Kevin Keegan and the building of the Entertainers with spectacular record signings one after the other was literally the most successful and exciting time in United's history for almost 70 years and therefore the bloody battle was justified.

United went from the brink of the old Third Division to runners-up in the Premier League and, had they won it rather than fall to Manchester United at the death, the Mags would have been changed forever.

However, the days of KK and signings like Alan Shearer, Peter Beardsley, Les Ferdinand, Andy Cole, Philippe Albert, David Ginola, Rob Lee and Tino Asprilla were so special, so spectacular, that they warmed the old heart of a dedicated Geordie.

For that rapid rise sparked by colossal signings a civil war was justified in my mind. It would never have happened without such drastic action.

xxxxx

GRAEME SOUNESS was an elegant assassin, a footballer

for all occasions. Stunningly handsome, he could ping the ball around with vision and sublime accuracy yet if a war erupted he was equally adroit with sword.

Souness fashioned his early promise at Middlesbrough and I got to know him well enough for him to give me a bell and urge me to try and get him a transfer to Newcastle.

Now this was around the time when Richard Dinnis gave way to Bill McGarry, which wasn't the most productive era for the Mags, and while United dithered over their options Liverpool moved in and all was lost.

Souness went on to win five League championships, three European Cups and four League Cups with the Reds so he had a lucky escape did he not? He could have been involved in glorious mediocrity upon the Tyne like the rest of us.

Of course he eventually ended up at Newcastle – but as manager.

United had a habit of recruiting world class footballers only not in their on-field pomp but as bosses when they brought nought but exasperation to the Toon Army.

I give you Ossie Ardiles, Kenny Dalglish, Ruud Gullit and Souness!

xxxxx

HE'S a proud Geordie presumably confused, as many were, by the sudden influx of French names into the Toon's ranks.

Thus when Glenn McCrory's partner Nicola – an Irish lass devoted to football but unfortunately that other United in Manchester – asked him how Newcastle were doing as he was flicking through Ceefax, our boxing hero went into overdrive. Squinting at the screen Glenn informed her triumphantly that they were indeed winning and began reading out the scorers.

Coming to the last one and triggered by the barrowload of Frenchmen so assembled he finished with: "Attent-daire 52 mins."

Nicola glanced up at the screen.

"Nah," she said, "that's attendance 52,000."

What a knock-out!

(above) Two men in the news: SuperMac helping me make a
advert for the *Chron*

(below left) Proudly holding the European Fairs Cup in 1969

(below right) Me and Mal taking centre stage on the TV floor

(Top) Some driver: Gazza chauffeuring me round Rome in a horse drawn buggy

(Left) Two young whippersnappers in dicky bows

(Above) I present a trophy to a baby faced youngster who grew up to be a sensation. His name? Paul Gascoigne

(*Above*) Rodney Bewes and myself cuddling our favourite Auntie Glad, mother of scriptwriter Ian La Frenais

(*Below*) Sharing a night of wine and roses with Ian

(*Above*) Survivors: Bjorn Borg and Gibbo at the Newcastle 900 celebrations

(*Right*) Keeping good company: with Peter Beardsley and his wife under the Eiffel Tower in Paris

(*Below*) I need a mike to get a word in edgeways with Cloughie

Above) The fabulous Wor Jackie and I sign copies of our book for young fans

Below) I must be pointing the way for Jackie to go and get himself a top coat

(Left) Brian Johnson, lead singer of AC/DC, plants his famous cap on my head and jumps on a chair so he can look down on me

(Below) Me and my Minder: Dennis Waterman, presumably in disguise with a beard

(Bottom) Sharing a settee with Mr Piano Man Elton John

Above left) With the Clown Prince of Soccer Len Shackleton

Top right) Modelling contrasting hairstyles: goalscorer supreme Alan Shearer with that other fella

Above right) I help a bleary looking Bestie

Below) Christmas party time: I get my hands on Budgie who is wearing a paper hat. Managers Denis Smith and Jim Smith look on with Chris Waddle

(Above) Playing a straight bat with Geoff Boycott

(Below) Newcastle United back my book signing session after winning the Fairs Cup. Back Row (left to right): John Craggs, coach Dave Smith, David Craig, Dave Elliott, and Ollie Burton. Front Row: Pop Robson, John Gibson, Bob Moncur, and Willie McFaul

When we brought
The Killer back
to town

TO HAVE been a teenager when rock 'n' roll exploded upon a bog-eyed world was to feel privileged. This was our time.

Music which had been melodic and romantic while in the hands of Sinatra, Crosby, Como and Fisher took on a more exciting raw edge.

Bill Haley, an ageing country and western singer with a kiss curl plastered over his forehead, recorded *Rock Around The Clock* which in 1955 swept America and then Britain. It stayed in the charts for one year solid.

Twelve months later Elvis Presley put sex into singing. Boasting sideburns and a smoulder, his *Heartbreak Hotel* bore the undeniable message: 'Lock up your daughters.'

There was a wildness, an abandonment about rockers. Jerry Lee Lewis almost smashed his piano leaping on the keyboard curly hair bouncing over his eyes, Little Richard was all baggy suit and a voice which screeched defiance, and Fats Domino found his thrill on *Blueberry Hill*.

However old you became, those early years belonged to you and your like. Therefore many moons later to work on a TV documentary about an original rock star, taking in a live concert as well, was a dream come true. It happened to me when we brought Jerry Lee back to the City Hall in Newcastle.

Now The Killer and the City Hall had history. In 1962 the guy who had been run out of the country for marrying his 13-year-old cousin defiantly returned to launch a new tour with Newcastle his first gig. How would he be received after scandalising a nation?

It was '58 when Jerry Lee had first come to Britain with Newcastle on his 37 tour dates but after only four gigs he was forced to flee. Maybe 13-year-old brides were fine in Mississippi law but certainly not over here. Back he came four years later, a rebel with a cause, and his City Hall reception was such that Lewis was carried from the stage on the shoulders of fans and into folklore. Such was the delirium Jerry Lee later wrote in his autobiography that this was his favourite show and Newcastle his favourite city. Cue Glenn McCrory and myself.

Glenn is of course a darned sight younger than me (most folk are) but he was brought up a bit of a rocker through his dad who had a mate called Freddie Fingers Lee. Fingers played just like Jerry Lee.

When McCrory was on Sky TV duty in Memphis for the Mike Tyson-Lennox Lewis fight he got into casual conversation with a couple of Scottish guys who had an intro to Jerry Lee. So Glenn found himself in the star's dressing room backstage at a concert given by the wild man who signed a copy of his *Greatest Hits* and thrust it into Geordie hands.

Much later in 2004 the Jocks were on about taking Lewis to Gleneagles to perform on a mini tour. Glenn, recalling Jerry's autobiography, suggested the City Hall was a must addition.

Hence there we were looking after the stuff of legends.

Naturally if we were doing the graft we wanted to turn it into a TV documentary. We were making a few at the time and this fitted in excellently.

Glenn organised an outside broadcast crew through his Sky connections and brought in the wonderful Mike Allen as director. He had worked with us on Liston-Tyson in Las Vegas.

When Jerry Lee arrived we duly deposited him in the Copthorne Hotel on Newcastle's Quayside and he immediately turned into Howard Hughes. A wild rocker beating up hotel rooms? A Killer? He was a recluse, man!

In four days he never left his confines once. Not once. Not for meals, for a look at the city he supposedly loved, or to meet his fans. Meals went in on a tray and he didn't come out.

What on earth was he doing? Playing video games almost non stop.

Meantime we were beavering away on the documentary. As the official reporter I was interviewing members of the Lewis band on camera. The likes of Jimmy Ripp, Kenny Lovelace, Charles White and Graham Knight. Good guys who gave a fascinating insight into life on the road and the stories of the stars.

Jerry Lee surfaced an hour before the concert and we transported him through town to the City Hall going behind stage with him.

The night was a real throwback. The place was packed and when the Lewis band went on as the opening act the aged rockers were bopping in the aisles. Tight trousers, drapes, bootlace ties, blue suede shoes and creaking limbs. What a combination.

Out came Jerry Lee to thunderous applause. His fingers were still amazingly supple, his voice strong and powerful. He rocked us through all his great hits.... *Great Balls of Fire, Whole Lotta Shakin' Goin' On, High School Confidential, What'd I Say*. He never drew breath between songs. It was dynamic, terrific, spine tingling. The only trouble was that he stayed but 35 minutes. No encore. When he walked off that was it. His band was left to close the show.

Afterwards I was back behind the mike interviewing stars like Chas and Dave who had travelled up from the smoke to see The Killer kill.

The documentary, I'm pleased to say, was well received. It's name? *Great Balls of Fire Pet* of course!

xxxxx

I SWEAR Rob Jones stands so tall he can rub shoulders with Earl Grey on the top of his monument. He is in fact 6ft 7in, which comes in handy when you are a centre-half.

I signed him for Gateshead in 2001 from a relegated Spennymoor because as a totem pole he dominated in the air at back and front. In 87 games for us Rob scored 19 times when a defender. See what I mean? The word quickly spread and the International Stadium became like a scouts convention. Every match they were there like vultures sitting on a fence.

I realised pretty quickly I needed to get Jones on a decent contract. So I locked him in the boardroom!

Why? Well it was pre-season and we were playing a mini tournament involving Scarborough, an ambitious club looking for a leg up. I knew they fancied our big fella.

When I got Rob in for talks immediately after a game I had to nip to the club office to get some paperwork and I didn't want Scarborough's chairman to just wander in upon their prey purely by accident. Hence the nifty key work.

I think Rob was a bit confused when I returned. Was the door stuck or locked chairman? Oh, stuck I think.

Anyway I got Jones on contract but Gateshead didn't cash in on him until after I had been made life president and left the boardroom. He was sold to Stockport County in the Football League far, far too cheaply at £5,000. What a missed opportunity with money so precious.

Rob Jones was the business. He went on to play for Grimsby Town, Hibernian, Scunthorpe United, Sheffield Wednesday and Doncaster Rovers. Career highlights included defeating Spurs' twin strikers Robbie Keane and Jermain Defoe and battling Newcastle's Alan Shearer in the 2004 Carling Cup with Grimsby and skippering Hibs to the Scottish League Cup when he scored their opening goal in the final.

I liked Rob, a great lad who made the very best of himself. It's good to play a small part in the development of guys like him.

When United stars had to buy underpants in a Cecil Gee shop

IT IS oft said, is it not, that Newcastle United are a football club of extremes. Nought is run of the mill. Dead ordinary.

That is as maybe but one astonishing week in 1972 beat all, taking us from the depths of despair to the heights of ecstasy.

First United were humiliated, disgraced before a watching nation, when they were kicked out of the FA Cup by a non-league team in Hereford who they had twice unsuccessfully attempted to beat.

However in the very next match they went off to Old Trafford and defeated Manchester United's superstars 2-0, a feat that took Newcastle 41 years to repeat. Now is that going from the cor blimey to the sublime? I rode that roller coaster with them all the way and boy it was some journey.

People tend to forget that United's shock loss to a Southern League Premier Division club was in a replay. Little Hereford actually came to St James' Park and snatched a 2-2 draw thanks to their player-manager Colin Addison.

Never mind Ronnie Radford's scorcher in Hereford's victory which has gone into folklore and is dragged out by the BBC every third round day much to the obvious irritation of us Geordies. Addison hit a 30-yard screamer up here which Malcolm Macdonald reckoned was the best goal he ever saw and SuperMac knew a few things about scoring.

Come the return and the country was in the grip of weather most foul rain, rain and more rain. The replay was postponed a couple of times until, with round four looming, Newcastle were suddenly put on a day to day alert.

We had all travelled into deepest Worcester for just an overnight stay but were to remain there from Monday to the Saturday waiting and waiting for a break in the weather.

Honest it was like a *Carry On* film. Pure slapstick. United's players had left Tyneside with only an overnight bag but were now in deep trouble and the local Cecil Gee shop was raided for shirts, underpants, socks, everything that required changing. They must have wondered what on earth was going on with desperate customers pouring in day upon day.

Training was restricted to light work-outs on a racecourse otherwise it was a matter of just hanging round the hotel. Boredom was our constant companion, relieved only by a fleeting visit to the local Dirty Duck pub for a couple of pints and a listen to the local country and western singer.

The third-round replay actually took place on round four Saturday and was to make the reputation of a certain young unknown commentator called John Motson.

Local farmers had laid straw on the pitch and only took it off on the Saturday morning, but the playing surface was still a quagmire. Nevertheless the Mags slaughtered Hereford's part-timers while passing up chance after chance until 10 minutes from time Viv Busby, on loan at the club, slung over a right-wing cross for SuperMac to head in at the back post. Thank goodness for that. Job done.

Except it wasn't. As time ebbed away a clearance from the back fell into midfield where the ball stuck in the clinging mud. John Tudor attempted to knock it to a support player but Radford closed and went right through him – a deep gash on his shin needed stitches after the game.

One touch by Radford and the ball hit a divot to stand up invitingly. He saw his opportunity, hit the ball with all his might, and Willie McFaul was clutching air.

We all know that Ricky George went on as a sub and scored the extra-time winner with a shot that passed through a forest of legs. What most didn't know was that Hereford's hero had been on the lash.

George was some character. The night before the tie he had gone to the local nightclub and wandered back to the hotel the wrong side of midnight. Jackie Milburn, who was with the Press pack, harangued him for being unprofessional.

"But Jackie," pleaded George in mitigation, "I'm a taxi driver, not a full-time footballer, and anyway I'm not playing!"

United's stars came across Ricky a couple of years later when, then a rep for Adidas, he delivered their FA Cup final boots to the team hotel. Oh, we lost again of course!

George was to become a good friend of John Motson and the two of them have travelled to many a reunion in Hereford for the '72 heroes. I got to know Motty well, too, and he always maintained that Newcastle made his broadcasting career. *Match of the Day* had planned a five-minute segment on their programme that night, fully expecting Newcastle to win, but elevated it to the main feature game when an upset materialised. Motty was elevated with it of course and a wondrous career as The Voice was under way.

"That cup-tie changed my life," John told me. "My boss at the Beeb Sam Leitch realised I could be trusted to commentate on a big match. If Newcastle hadn't lost I might have been the one who was lost forever."

For me trudging back to Tyneside with a case full of dirty washing and a bag full of broken dreams was nothing short of a disaster. We were a public laughing stock once again and a week later ran out at Old Trafford to chants of "Hereford, Hereford" from a 44,983 crowd.

Man U were led by their Three Musketeers George Best, Bobby Charlton and Denis Law and no doubt thought this was a cakewalk.

However Newcastle are always best against the best and vulnerable when facing small fry. By half-time they were a goal to the good and 2-0 victors 45 minutes later. Since that day February 12, 1972 Newcastle never won away to Man U, at least until nearly every visiting team did in 2013-14.

The historic goals were scored by John Tudor and Stewart Barrowclough and nine of those disgraced at Hereford kept their places. The only changes were Barrowclough for Busby, who had been packed off home after the cup-tie, and Tommy Gibb for Irving Nattrass, who got on as a sub.

XXXXX

FOOTBALL attracts sponsors like moths around a light.

There are of course the good, the bad, and the indifferent. Hennessy Cognac most certainly fell into the first category.

Together with the *Chron* they used to back Player of the Month awards for all three top North East clubs and then, as the grand finale, a grand Player of the Year do at the Civic Centre in Newcastle.

That culminated in a wonderful weekend trip to the most fascinating of cities Paris where our winner was treated like the king he was.

I made that journey with both Chris Waddle and Peter Beardsley, most worthy winners, both exceptionally talented, England regulars and entertainers par excellence.

We would fly from Newcastle on the Friday afternoon linking up with Hennessy's top man Phillip Juniper and his wife Kay at Heathrow, have a succulent dinner at a swish restaurant on the Champs-Elysées that night, go shopping and sightseeing Saturday daytime before ending up at the spectacular Lido Nightspot, and then do a final tour of the city on the Sunday before flying back home.

With Chris Waddle and wife Lorna we indulged ourselves. We walked the Champs-Elysées, climbed the Eiffel Tower, visited Montmartre with its quaint cafes and pavement artists, and took a boat down the Seine.

On our particular night at the Lido we even met the Irish lady who formed the famed Bluebell Girls, 75-year-old Margaret Kelly, and we persuaded Chris to do a high kicking routine with her for some publicity shots.

This was a lad I first met when I had no idea he was bound for undying fame.

United's winger John Connolly and myself went along

to Clark Chapmans to present their end-of-season awards, something I did a thousand times across the North East.

A lot of handshakes, a few quick photographs, and Conn and myself were off into town for one or two lagers. Never thinking much about the do. Except that, several years later, Waddle produced a slightly crumpled photograph of the Clarke Chapman's team group with Connolly and me in the back row.

He pointed to a youngster in row one. It was a very young Chris Waddle long before United rescued him from being a sausage seasoner in a local factory and put him on the road to stardom. From an award winner in Gateshead to an award winner in Paris. Quite a jump for a Geordie lad.

Beardsley was the same. No apprenticeship, no proper grooming. He signed for Carlisle United late in his teens because Bob Moncur, their manager, spotted in him what others had missed.

A year after going to Paris with Waddle I repeated the trip with Peter and Sandra Beardsley. Such was Peter's considerable standing, already being an England international, that as we strolled round the packed roadside cafes of Montmartre he was recognised in a foreign land and asked for his autograph.

These were special players, gifted players, Geordie players. Yet United in a very short space of time sold them, and another in the same mould in Paul Gascoigne. And then were surprised when they were relegated!

The World Cup winning failure

UNITED'S hordes have always adored their centre-forwards who wear the black and white with pride and a dash of derring-do.

Done Up To The Nines could well be Newcastle's theme tune after the *Blaydon Races*.

Those who adorn the famed shirt are put on a pedestal – but those who fail are hounded out of town.

Unbelievably in one case the Mags had the most decorated No.9 possible and supposedly the worst of all time in one controversial bundle.

May I present Stephane Guivarc'h, World Cup winning centre-forward who was voted the Premier League's worst ever striker by a national newspaper for his brief but disastrous spell on Tyneside.

Let me go back to 1998, the year it all happened for a soccer player originally intriguing in our parts only for having an apostrophe in his surname.

As usual I was sent by the *Chron* to cover the World

Cup finals, this time in France, a trip heightened in breathless excitement by the fact that the Gallic No.9 had just signed for the Toon. The gathering anticipation of seeing a great new Geordie hero before he reached the coal face was palpable.

Early in my excursions I was having a chilled wine in the Press hotel when I was introduced to a guy who was a football scout with West Ham. At the time he was doing a Graham Carr i.e. trawling the hinterlands of France looking for a pebble that would turn out to be a diamond.

Oh, I thought, a nice story coming up. The fella must have seen Guivarc'h and he could wax lyrical, which would go down a treat back home.

The scout was Peter Storrie who went on to become chief executive at Portsmouth during the FA Cup winning reign of Harry Redknapp.

"So what about Guivarc'h?" I enquired, my pen poised for the avalanche of gushing words about to pour forth. Tell me a Storrie!

Except the words weren't glorious. They were critical.

According to Peter our bright new signing hadn't enough about him, physically and talent wise, to cut it in the Premier League. He may have scored goals for Auxerre and won baubles, he may have been about to lead the line of a hugely talented French side, but the stunning prediction was that he wouldn't become a Wor Jackie, SuperMac or Alan Shearer.

Dearie me, story gone. I put away my notebook and cancelled the piece back home. No one would wish to read that our new partner for Shearer was destined for nothingsville. I prayed West Ham's talent spotter was wrong. He wasn't of course. I sat in gathering amazement as France stormed through the World Cup to the final itself and Guivarc'h, a centre-forward remember, failed to score a solitary single goal.

Had the No.9 of any World Cup winning side ever drawn a blank every time he walked out onto the pitch, and at a home tournament to boot? Sir Geoff Hurst must have winced.

When Guivarc'h at last wore the stripes he hadn't earned my worst fears were confirmed. He might have scored a scruffy goal on his debut against Liverpool but he played only four times as our leader. Bought by Kenny Dalglish who promptly left, Guivarc'h was dispatched to the scrapheap by Ruud Gullit.

The World Cup final itself was sensational not because of the winning No.9 Guivarc'h but Brazil's attack leader Ronaldo, a goalscoring machine as sleek as a Rolls-Royce.

Drama, controversy, confusion, mystery… it had it all and more. Only it was before kick-off and not afterwards.

As always I was early into my seat in the Stade de France and just as well. When the teamsheets arrived 72 minutes before the off Ronaldo wasn't in coach Mario Zagallo's side. Red alert, mass panic.

There was absolutely no explanation though we all naturally thought an injury kept secret on the very biggest of days was to blame. An ankle injury was the first guess, then an upset stomach was put forward as the reason.

However half an hour later another Brazilian teamsheet was hurriedly handed out and this time Ronaldo was in his customary position of centre-forward. What the hell was happening? Rumours of a dispute within the Brazilian camp were fuelled when the team failed to emerge for their pre-match warm-up.

This wasn't any old game, it was the World Cup final. And Ronaldo wasn't any old player but a matchwinner in canary yellow.

The game itself hardly lived up to its dramatic prelude, Zinedine Zidane rising twice above the Brazilian defence to give France a 2-0 lead before half-time.

Brazil tried in vain to stage a recovery after France's Marcel Desailly was sent off on 68 minutes but it was Emmanuel Petit who scored next to spark wild celebrations on the Champs-Elysées.

By the by. What had happened to Ronaldo? The whole world wanted to know. Finally team doctor Lidio Toledo revealed the striker had been rushed to hospital after suffering a convulsion in his sleep but cleared to play after neurological and cardiac tests.

The most dramatic account of what occurred came from Ronaldo's room-mate Roberto Carlos.

He told us: "Ronaldo was scared about what lay ahead. The pressure had got to him and he couldn't stop crying.

"If anything it got worse because, at about four o'clock, he started being sick. That's when I called the team doctor and told him to get over to our room as fast as he could."

Ronaldo was taken to hospital during the afternoon and his place in the team given to Edmundo.

When Zagallo addressed his side in the hotel he had reminded his players about 1962 when Brazil won the World Cup without the injured Pele. However Ronaldo had later arrived at the Stade de France and declared himself fit to play.

If Ronaldo was the talking point across the globe and Zidane the goalscoring hero, what of Guivarc'h?

Well, he didn't even last until the final whistle to celebrate on the pitch. He was subbed for Christophe Dugarry in the 66th minute.

My conversation with Peter Storrie had sadly been spot on the button.

XXXXX

MY HOW times have changed... but is it all for the better?

Maybe there was a naivety, if not an innocence, about football in the Swinging Sixties.

When United lifted their first and last European trophy in 1969 I had already began writing the *Newcastle United FC Story*. My accidental timing couldn't have been better with a chapter added on each round of the Fairs Cup up to its glorious conclusion in Budapest.

So when the book hit the shelves a short while later the Geordie response was total. There were queues round the book store in the shadow of Grey's Monument where I was doing a launch.

Not surprising when you realise the situation. Every single player in United's squad was present. We all sat in a long line with the book and me in the middle – oh, and the Fairs Cup itself at one end gleaming in all its splendour.

Could you imagine that today? And it was on a match morning, a Saturday before a 3pm kick off at

St James' Park! The club wouldn't allow such an imposition nowadays and rightly so. In any case the whole team wouldn't turn out in support of a mere hack.

What's more the Euro heroes didn't get a bent penny for their efforts. All they got was a party down at my gaff paid for by a delighted publisher who had travelled up from London to witness the occasion and stood counting the coin.

I also ghosted the autobiography of United skipper Bobby Moncur, who had notched a hat-trick over the two-legged final. He turned up at my house in Whitley Bay a few days after arriving back from Hungary with the Fairs Cup lying on the back seat of his car.

The second leg was held in June, which meant decent weather, and Bob strode out into our back garden, plonked the cup on the lawn, and we all enjoyed a few light ales while my daughter Sally played with her shiny new toy.

Yeah, times have changed all right.

Reporting the
hard way

**NEW TECHNOLOGY has revolutionised the world
of communications.**

What has occurred during my working life has been
unbelievable, unthinkable when I first sallied forth covering
the might of Hexham Hearts for the *Hexham Courant* with a
week to stew over the composition of my report.

Now anywhere in the world at the touch of a keypad I
can send my story winging its way into the *Chronicle* offices.
I have done so from Australia and Japan, Mexico and Los
Angeles. Time stands still, if it's 4am back home no matter.
Press a button and go to bed.

However when I first started out on the United beat it was
so very different. It was literally the dark ages in comparison.
Filing copy to head office was an endurance test.

Imagine a Premier League ground without a phone at
your elbow. Impossible, isn't it? Blow me, now there are mini
TV screens where you can instantly view the replay of a
goal for offside etc.

Yet at Leeds United – the home of stars like Billy Bremner, Johnny Giles, Allan Clarke and Jack Charlton – they didn't even have phones in the Press box. Visiting hacks doing a running report for the football edition that night had to write it out in long hand, pass it to an eager kid wishing to earn a couple of pennies, and he would run down a flight of a dozen stairs into the Press room where there was an open phone line to Newcastle. He would hurriedly phone over the copy then hare back for the next sheet.

Honestly, I would wait with baited breath for the fixtures to come out in the despairing hope that United would be playing at Leeds either on Boxing Day when we didn't print any papers, or on a midweek night when there was no runner for *The Pink*.

Fledgling days in Europe on Fairs Cup duty were even worse. When we drew Inter Milan it looked a dream trip… only we stayed in the little village of Ispra on Lake Maggiore in a hotel which had only one line either in or out. Only one in the whole hotel.

Charming with a dozen or so Press men desperate to file Joe Harvey's latest words of wisdom to a waiting audience back home. To make matters worse the whole telephone system collapsed when there was mist over the lake and we hit two misty days out of three.

My fixed time calls came anything up to two and a half hours late and with a deadline to meet that was ridiculous. Inevitably I was cut off two or three times, blood pressure going through the roof. I finished off looking like Captain Beetroot!

My worst experience was when I couldn't get put through from the *Chronicle* switchboard to the copy room without losing the line. One of the girls eventually had to go downstairs onto the switchboard and take my call there with an ordinary phone held against her ear trying to type at the same time rather than wearing an earpiece.

In the end, *Fawlty Towers* having taken over, I finished off sending my stories to Tyne Tees Television on the back of their reporter's call and they kindly phoned it on to my office in the Bigg Market.

We thought we had experienced all that is bad – until Newcastle drew Pecsi Dozsa, a little club buried in the backwaters of Hungary. No phones in the hotel bedrooms once more. The travel company really knew how to look after the needs of the Press. Worse for me in particular, the kick off was at 1.30 in the afternoon because the club had no floodlights which meant a runner for the *Chron*.

No lights? They had no Press box either (think of that at a club which had qualified for Europe). So we all ended up sitting at little round bar tables on a running track, mine supporting a phone for my running report.

I managed it somehow after getting a line back home and then dodging the mighty tackles of the likes of John McNamee. At one time he took the ball and the legs of a Pecsi player in one ferocious tackle, sliding over the touchline and under my table which rocked violently as I desperately tried to continue dictating to a copy girl in Newcastle.

What a match that was. I wanted it over as quickly as possible due to the testing circumstances but inevitably it went to extra-time, and finally a penalty shoot-out. Even then, after a longish delay, players were brought back from the dressing room to complete five stipulated penalties.

United, having missed all three of their early spot kicks, had departed the field in humiliation.

Just to rub salt into gaping wounds I had to report in great detail that United had been kicked out of Europe by one of the minnows. Worth a long day's work, wasn't it?

United had won 2-0 at home in the first leg with big Wyn Davies netting twice. Good enough? Probably we thought.

The town of Pecs had no airport so we flew into Budapest, stayed overnight in the same hotel occupied when the Fairs Cup was so gloriously won, and the following day made the 100 mile plus trip south. We spent four hours in a vehicle better suited to transporting cattle to market.

With no hotel big enough to take the whole party we were split into two. The only trouble was ours had no restaurant!

On a pitch more like the Town Moor than Wembley an atrocious United were 2-0 down after 90 minutes, their opponents hung on during extra-time, and in the penalty shoot-out somehow roared into a 3-0 lead. Newcastle were out and the players trudged into the dressing room, heads hanging in shame.

However the referee, who must have been a masochist, insisted on all five kicks being taken and so Newcastle sent out the two players who hadn't yet taken off their playing kit, Willie McFaul and Frank Clark.

Meanwhile delirious Pecsi fans, who had never dreamed of triumph, were going loopy on the track. Everyone wanted to shake me by the hand (I wanted to shake them by the throat) and one nutcase kept pouring popcorn into the mouthpiece of my phone while I tried to continue talking. Eventually Ivor Broadis, the old Newcastle and England inside-forward, rescued me from the mob. Reporting on Newcastle has always been rather eventful!

XXXXX

WHAT was the best team I've ever seen? Kevin Keegan's Entertainers weren't bad. Neither were the Manchester United of Best, Law and Charlton. Or the Liverpool European Cup winners of old. However none can quite compare to Brazil of 1970. What sheer joy, what pleasure, what wallowing.

I saw every match live that the magical Brazilians played during Mexico '70 apart from the quarter-final when I was in Leon for the England-Germany game.

What's more I travelled down from Guadalajara to Mexico City for the final on the same aeroplane as Brazil's superstars, a rare privilege. Pele stood the whole flight having his photo taken and signing autographs.

The essence of Brazil's side were the Famous Five attackers. Poetry in motion. Take a bow gentlemen: Jairzinho was a panther-like player who attacked with grace and venom down the right; Gerson the dapper, balding midfield master who made them tick; the ever willing Tostao played despite his vision in one eye being badly impaired; Pele the greatest footballer of all time, the only one better than George Best; and Rivelino, he of the incredible banana free-kick.

They reckoned that England's '70 side was even better than the one which won the World Cup four years previously but they still lost to Brazil under the murderous midday sun burning out of Mexico's blue skies.

When the IRA were to shoot George Best

SOMETIMES, only sometimes, a footballer transcends his station and attains pop idol status, adored by squealing girls.

One was, of course, George Best. Another David Beckham. I knew them both and witnessed the adulation first hand.

George WAS the Best. Roguishly handsome, a Beatle in all but name, he was in his pomp a wondrous player and a devastating lad on the pull. The trouble was booze came with the birds and it was a heady mix.

I worked with him many times doing talk-ins across our patch. He was either a glorious storyteller or an absolute sloshed nightmare.

We did a dinner together in Chester-le-Street and Bestie ought to have had a red light on his head signalling danger.

He arrived late, inevitably with his latest bimbo in tow, and fixed me with glazed eyes and a manic grin. It was apparent to all that he had been on the sauce.

However instead of trying to wean him away from the booze our hosts readily bought him another shot. By the time I sat next to him on the top table George could hardly speak, yet he kept on drinking throughout the courses even when I tried to hide the wine bottle and substitute tap water. We were to do a question and answer session rather than Best launching into an after-dinner speech, his choice, but while I produced plenty of questions there were no coherent answers. Just a slurred Irish burr and a few hand gestures.

The questions got longer and the answers shorter.

I was desperately uneasy and eventually had to give up any attempt at conning us through the session.

Remember Terry Wogan having to wrap up his live chat show interview with a distinctly drunk George? I felt a bit like Terence. Being a sober sidekick ain't a lot of fun.

However on another occasion in Newcastle's city centre George was in sparkling form. Witty and sharp, cutting and funny.

He naturally regaled us with the story of the Irish waiter who brought the champagne to his bedroom where Miss World Mary Stavin was lying on the bed in a negligée with several thousand pounds of gambling winnings littering what space was left around her.

"George," said the concerned waiter, "where did it all go wrong?" The story was new then and so extremely funny it went into legend.

When in a nightclub Bestie would merely stand at the end of the bar and girls would be lining up to tap him. Honestly, often he would rather natter to us guys about football.

I was at St James' Park reporting on Newcastle United v

Manchester United the day the IRA were supposed to shoot George stone dead. Yeah, truthfully!

It was in October of 1971 at the height of the troubles in Northern Ireland and someone claiming to be from the IRA told police that Best would be shot if he played.

Man U manager Frank O'Farrell gave George the option of pulling out of the match but that of course would have opened the door for every crank north, south, east and west to make similar phone calls in the future. Bestie could have ended up never playing again.

So, no, he said. He would play.

The trouble was that the team coach which had been parked in the hotel's underground car park had been broken into overnight, which only served to heighten tension. Two detectives eventually boarded the coach with Bestie, who wasn't allowed in his usual window seat in case anyone took a pot shot at him. In fact when it pulled into St James' Park George was lying in the aisle well out of sight.

Police were everywhere as the teams ran out scouring the rooftops with high powered binoculars.

Bestie told me later he had never ran about so much in his life. You know, a moving target and all that.

Typically he scored the only goal of the game.

Afterwards while the police gave Manchester United an escort out of town, Newcastle boss Joe Harvey was lamenting George's winner.

"I wish they had shot the little bugger," he said in the Press conference amid nervous laughter. When George found out later he guffawed. "Thanks, Joe," he said. "But mine was the only shot on target all afternoon!" Football humour is no respecter of the politically correct. It had been a crank call but who was to know at the time? George Best could easily have been the juiciest of targets for the IRA seeking a propaganda coup.

Another Man U star many years later, David Beckham, became showbiz just like Mr B. However instead of Miss World he went out with and married a Posh Spice Girl. Though Becks never put it about in the very Best of styles he still had a legion of girl fans, especially in the Far East.

When I travelled with England to the 2002 World Cup finals in Japan I witnessed mass hysteria at an unprecedented level for a footballer. Beckham was mobbed whenever he appeared in public. Even going to daily training required a Herculean effort. At both the hotel and training ground legions of Japanese girls carrying huge pics of Becks lined the pavement spilling into the road much to the annoyance of passing traffic. When they couldn't get to their hero some of them would descend upon whoever was vaguely connected to the England camp. And that included me.

I lost count of the number of fans (yes, ladies' fans and, no, I don't know why) that were thrust into my hands with messages written on them and a plea for me to pass them on to England's skipper. Some are even lying in the back of a cupboard upstairs in my house right now. I never got round to chucking 'em out.

Naturally I got to know quite a few of the England players over a long period of time covering World Cup and European Championship matches and Becks was one of them.

I can honestly say that he's a lovely guy, warm and

courteous, with not a hint of snooty superstar about him.
I like him a lot. Different from George. Oh, very different.
But both likeable in their own ways.

XXXXX

UNITED always had a full quota of chanters on hand in
the old days just in case an impromptu party was called.

The most obvious night of wild celebrations came when
the European Fairs Cup was secured in Hungary's capital
city of Budapest on the blue Danube. A star performer was
amongst us of course – singer David MacBeth, who ran
Grey's Club where many of the Newcastle players used to
accompany me for a night out after Saturday matches.

David was a real Frank Sinatra type, smooth and easy with
a wonderful voice. He had a big hit with *Mr Blue* and toured
with the Beatles and Roy Orbison which is not a bad gig.

Not many people realised that he was once on Newcastle's
books. He loved his football and was in Budapest along with
United's army of fans.

MacBeth was particularly close to Jack Charlton, later
manager of Newcastle, and used to take his voice and stylish
act on many trips with the Republic of Ireland squad.

Anyway come June of 1969 MacBeth led the singing
late into the night with the likes of myself providing an
inadequate chorus. However there was good support –
Frank Clark was a terrific guitarist whose party piece was
Meggy Thoo (*Peggy Sue* but with a slight lisp) while big John
McNamee had a magnificent falsetto voice that belied his
size and aggressive play.

Better than Colemanballs

SOME celebs can brighten up a room just by leaving it.

Not Bobby Robson. He lit up the place like a Christmas tree, all twinkling lights and warm glow.

Sir Bob was universally loved, a man in his element when surrounded by those who care as passionately as he did about sport.

He achieved virtually everything in football, both as a player of international stature and manager, but he also harboured the warmest of glows for cricket.

Many a joyous summer afternoon was spent watching his beloved Durham at Chester-le-Street.

As befits a man of his standing he was invited down to Lord's, cricket's ancestral home, as an after-dinner speaker. Oh how proud he was.

When it came to rising to his feet he held his audience spellbound. Warmth radiated from his every pore.

"I was privileged to play for and manage England's

football team," he beamed, chest puffed out. "I only wish I could have done the same in cricket. To have walked out here at Lord's as captain of England would have had me bursting with pride.

"To do it even a few times like Geoff Boycott and John Edrich would have been wonderful but imagine being the regular leader of your country like Len Hutton, Colin Cowdrey, Ted Dexter, Mike Brearley, and … Saddam Hussein!"

Cue stunned silence. Had the wrong bloke been captured and pronounced guilty in Iraq?

Then the penny dropped. Bobby meant Nasser Hussain.

A few sniggers were followed by warm applause. The man could walk on water.

And, no, it wasn't old age that prompted Robson to mix up names. Senility wasn't the guilty party.

Bobby would get names wrong even when a young manager at Ipswich.

Watching a practice match one of his players, blessed with much talent, kept choosing an option his manager didn't like.

"Sykesy," Robson kept bellowing. No one took any notice. "Sykesy." Again no response.

Eventually the coach stopped the session as Bobby appeared on the verge of a red-faced fit.

Syksey, it turned out upon inquiry, was Eric Gates and not Eric Sykes the comedian!

When Shola Ameobi was famously asked what Bobby called him, he replied deadpan: "Carl Cort."

Jack Charlton, he of World Cup fame, was much the same

when it came to players' names. Chris Waddle and Peter Beardsley were Big Laird and Little Laird while his new centre-forward signing at Newcastle, Tony Cunningham, was referred to as Blackie Milburn.

Politically incorrect it most certainly was but then Big Jack was a law unto himself, a rough diamond with not a racist bone in his body, and Tony, knowing it was never meant to be offensive, often regaled all himself with the tale amid wide smiles.

Bobby was of course the kindest of men. If he knew you and liked you then his world was yours.

I worked with Robson from his early days at Ipswich, through his time as England manager and onwards.

Often he would motor all the way up to the North East from East Anglia just to do a talk-in with me in a pub or social club in deepest Tyneside. Can you imagine Fabio Capello, Terry Venables, or Sven-Goran Eriksson doing that? That's how much he liked talking shop to his own folk.

When he took self-imposed exile in Europe after his England experiences I got in touch and asked if I could fly out to see him. A Geordie with the same interests. Of course I could.

Bobby was boss of Porto at the time which meant several changes of plane. Newcastle to London, London to Lisbon, and finally Lisbon to Oporto. Inevitably my luggage got lost.

No matter, when Bobby heard he immediately came over to my hotel with armfuls of gear...all official Porto attire. Club blazer and tie, club shirt and so forth.

I walked round the city for the next three days like some celeb, an Englishman brought over by "Meester Robson" to presumably impart some tactical wisdom to his players. I met Bobby's interpreter more than once, on the training ground and in restaurants where we enjoyed dinner.

A handsome man, bronzed and with a twinkle in his eye, I thought no more about him until several years later when I rummaged through my old photos to confirm my belief. It was Jose Mourinho.

Bobby and I sat one afternoon on the seafront watching the Atlantic crash against the rocks billowing spray. In such pleasant surroundings Bobby opened his heart.

He had recently suffered his first encounter with cancer and his thoughts about us all being vulnerable came tumbling out. Life was to be embraced, to be enjoyed and treasured.

"I'll beat it," Robson maintained, clenching his fist. "I'll beat it." He did for an awful long time but eventually, inevitably, a big heart was stilled.

Fast forward to just before he died and, totally lacking hair and looking gaunt but with defiance still shining through, we talked again in a hotel lounge on the Quayside. This time it was of his Foundation, his legacy.

I was privileged to attend the memorial service in his honour at Durham Cathedral in September of 2009. It was to be our final farewell to a pitman's son.

If this mighty cathedral which took 40 years to complete has witnessed much down the vast passage of time, rarely if ever can football's royalty have passed through its doors in such vast numbers. Sir Alex Ferguson, Gary Lineker, Gazza, Paul Mariner, Steve McClaren, Pep Guardiola, Alan Shearer, David Seaman, Sven-Goran Eriksson, Sir Bobby

Charlton, Shay Given, David Moyes, Sir Trevor Brooking, Peter Beardsley, Jermaine Jenas. The list was endless.

My tribute report in the *Chronicle* the next day was written with a tear in the eye and as it turned out was to play a significant part in me winning a national sportswriter of the year award. He was a helpful friend to the end was Wor Bobby.

XXXXX

COLEMANBALLS became so famous books were sold by the shedload over any Christmas.

However Bobby Robson could match anything concocted by the Beeb's finest and did so on many occasions involving his much loved Newcastle players.

When Bobby first arrived Alan Shearer, who had a poor relationship with the previous manager Ruud Gullit, was playing with his back to goal and not looking anything like the explosive England goalscorer we knew.

Robson changed his body position, getting him side on and with it his impact upon a game. He explained it to me while stressing how important it had been to win over his skipper.

"Alan Shearer has done very well for us, considering his age," said Mr R. "We have introduced some movement into his game because he has got two good legs now. He used to play with one leg."

Well, er, we kind of know what you mean Bobby!

It worked almost immediately anyway because in Bobby's first home game against Sheffield Wednesday, Shearer scored a sensational five goals in an 8-0 rout. On Craig Bellamy, an explosive partner who famously had a big run-in with Shearer, United's manager informed us: "He's the only man I know who could start an argument with himself."

Robson was a great admirer of Gary Speed and scathing of anyone who suggested his sell by date was rapidly approaching.

"We can't replace Gary Speed," snorted Bob on one such occasion. "Where do you get an experienced player like him with a left foot and a head? Gary Speed has never played better, never looked fitter, never been older."

Laurent Robert could be more of a problem – terrific one day, frustrating the next. This was a frustrating day.

"In the first half he took a corner, a poor corner, which hit the first defender," said Robson, "and it took him 17 minutes to get back to the halfway line."

Ever the gentleman, Bobby loved to reminisce and would often take a whimsical look back over his playing career.

"Denis Law once kicked me at Wembley in front of the Queen in an international. I mean, no man is entitled to do that, really."

The look of sadness said it all.

When the Lord
was caught out

LORD WESTWOOD was a man with a razor sharp wit, a captivating conversationalist who was an outstanding after-dinner speaker.

He also cut a distinctive figure with a patch over his left eye (lost in a car crash) and snowy white hair.

A director of Hornby Railways amongst a host of companies, he will be remembered most for his chairmanship of Newcastle United.

For 18 years he held power at St James' Park including when United won their last meaningful trophy, the European Fairs Cup of 1969.

However it was the manner of Lord Westwood's departure that caused controversy, a double whammy if you like that brought some outrage amongst fans.

Back in 1981 when United were in dire straits, each director was asked to put up a £16,000 guarantee to help the club's finances. Lord Westwood had just been hit with a big financial loss following the stock market collapse of

DCM, Europe's leading toy company of which he was chairman, and wishing to protect his family's inheritance he refused and quit the board.

However his timing was delayed to allow him to carry out what would have to be his final job as president of the Football League – presenting the League Cup to the winners of the Liverpool v West Ham final at Wembley.

However in an ironic twist the match ended 1-1 and by the time the replay came about on April 1 at Villa Park Lord Westwood was no longer League president and therefore unable to carry out the ceremony. Liverpool won 2-1 by the way.

To the thinking of some fans angered by Westwood's refusal to help bail out United after living a privileged life in the boardroom, it was poetic justice.

Newcastle in those days used their close proximity to the border to raid Scotland for their footballers. Lord Westwood's cousin Hal Stewart ran Morton and such a link inevitably brought about business, notably the signing of Preben Arentoft who was to star and score in the European Fairs Cup final against Ujpest Dozsa.

I remember Benny telling me of those deals – the first from his Danish club Bronshoj to Morton and then Morton to Newcastle.

Morton, he claimed, made a fortune picking up players on the cheap and flogging them for a healthy profit. As an amateur club Bronshoj didn't get a penny for Benny, with Stewart telling him from the off that the whole idea was to sell him on.

Arentoft wanted full-time football so that suited him fine

and a secret meeting was set up in Carlisle when United did a deal with club and player. Benny actually ended up as a player with Morton AND United for a fortnight!

That was because at the time there was a ban on foreign players coming into the Football League but United director Wilf Taylor, a League vice president dispatched to Carlisle, had the inside track on such things and he believed he had discovered a loophole. Arentoft had lived in Britain for more than three years and had married a Scottish lass. As such he would be acceptable.

At a meeting of the League Management Committee a fortnight later Arentoft's registration was accepted. With Lord Westwood and Taylor batting for Newcastle, what a surprise!

Inevitably I had my run-ins with Lord Bill as any self respecting hack must challenge football chairmen if he does his job properly, but I still found him an extremely witty raconteur. When leaving United he invited me round to his house in Gosforth where he presented me with several specially produced books from his time as Football League president, vice chairman of the Football Association, and service on the UEFA professional committee.

I also got to know his eldest son Gavin well – he actually sided once with the rebels against the board run by his father!

William Westwood, 2nd Baron Westwood, was born on Christmas Day 1907 – did he look a bit like Santa Claus with his snowy hair? – and died a month short of his 85th birthday. His life was certainly colourful if controversial.

xxxxx

SUCH is Tyneside's deep-rooted passion for sport that even the most sad and personal of occasions can be infiltrated with a touch of outrageous humour.

I remember when I was getting divorced attending the court with my wife. After the usual proceedings I was given a message that the judge would like to see me in chambers.

In I went with my now ex-wife not far behind.

"Oh," said he who must be obeyed nodding towards my former beloved, "you may go if you wish. This doesn't involve you." However curiosity being what it is amongst the female of the species she declined his kind offer and decided to listen to the spiel.

After the courtesy of asking if we were both satisfied with the financial arrangements (too late if we weren't) the judge turned to me and said: "I know who you are of course.

"I'm a great rugby man but unfortunately I haven't a ticket for England's game with Scotland at Murrayfield and I wondered if you could help!"

I could see the clerk's shoulders heaving with suppressed laughter.

After light heartedly suggesting I would have looked for a better financial arrangement had I known his dependency upon me, I said I would do what I could.

"Good, I'm at Blyth tomorrow – just phone me at this number," he replied with a beaming smile. "The clerk can get a message to me and I can adjourn the hearing to take your call." Honestly, not a word of a lie.

Duncan Madsen, who used to play for Gosforth's highly successful John Player Cup side, was my rugby man at the *Chron* and as a former Scottish international he qualified automatically for tickets. I asked Dunc if he could help and he did. One satisfied judge!

Luckily my ex-wife and I remained good friends. We actually went round the corner for a coffee straight from the "gizz a ticket" meeting and had a good laugh about it.

XXXXX

WHEN an unknown local with absolutely no playing background attempts to revolutionise the way footballers train he inevitably provokes as many sneers as plaudits.

So it was with Lennie Heppell, a silver-haired nightclub owner from the market town of Hexham who walked into the suspicious world of top class soccer and suggested such revolutionary ideas that people of influence were left scratching their heads.

Lennie was a ballroom champion along with his wife Molly and his only affiliation to football was that United's European Fairs Cup winning hero Bryan Pop Robson married his daughter Maureen.

Heppell had made a name for himself tripping the light fantastic on telly's popular pop show *Six Five Special* as well as at his nightclub the Fandango in Hexham, where I worked on my first newspaper the *Courant*.

What Lennie had of course was balance and rhythm and I remember him telling me that despite all his promise Pop could be an even better player if he walked and ran correctly. So he took Bryan onto Sele Park at Hexham and down by the riverside to work with him one on one.

When United boss Joe Harvey found out he went berserk.

Joe was old school and a balance expert to him ought to have been working with ballet dancers not bruising footballers.

There were others whose minds were more open to new teachings. Revolutionary Manchester City coach Malcolm Allison, who had won the old First Division championship at St James' Park, was one. Brian Clough another.

West Ham, a club graced by Pop of course, were also willing to listen and once World Cup legend Bobby Moore reacted without rancour to the bravely voiced opinion that he "ran as though he was supported by a coat hanger" (i.e. stiffly upright) others of considerable pedigree like Trevor Brooking embraced the Hexham guru.

Thus Lennie's reputation spread like wildfire and he worked with such diverse personalities as Frank Bruno, Steffi Graf and Bjorn Borg. All of a sudden Lennie wasn't a crank but a maestro!

Indeed where Harvey had told Heppell to take a runner, Kevin Keegan when Newcastle manager invited him in three times a week to work with the players.

I spent many an afternoon listening to Lennie's theories produced with infectious enthusiasm.

Heppell was way ahead of his time but how on earth, I asked him, did he know he could transform what he did on the dance floor to the football pitch or tennis court.

"Because I coached my sister Philomena and daughter Maureen to become champions at table tennis," he told me. Indeed Maureen went on to become an England international.

Sadly Lennie passed away in May of 2009 after a good innings at the age of 89. I miss him.

Fireball in the sun

THE Atlantic Ocean was pounding the shore of arguably the most famous beach on planet earth outside my hotel on Florida's sunshine coast. All was well with the world – for the moment.

It was along the vast flat expanses of Daytona Beach that Sir Malcolm Campbell had attempted to set a world land speed record many moons ago. *Baywatch*, too, was filmed there on occasions and scores of Pamela Anderson lookalikes, all golden locks and silicone, were bouncing along the strip caught up in the glamour of the Daytona 24-hour race.

It was early 1996 and I was living amongst international jet setters because, believe it or not, Newcastle United had entered the most gruelling of endurance races.

The Lister Storm GTI team was carrying the black and white colours of our beloved and were backed on the trip by Premier League supremo Rick Parry as well as a couple of Newcastle directors. And where United went the *Chron* liked to be, so there was I.

The race itself is much more spectacular than its big brother Formula One. The banking on the Daytona oval which can accommodate 150,000 race fanatics is so steep that if a driver dropped below 70mph his car would slide down the track.

Daytime temperatures of 80 degrees gave way to cool night air creating vivid pictures in the darkness as cars, headlights on, raced up and down the vast banks like demented flies on a window.

Inevitably the tiredness that eats away at drivers over the 24 hours was a major concern for the Geordie team. Even though the wheelmen had an hour on and two hours off as three co-drivers took turns, the relentless pressure made the body feel it could take no more punishment. It's not just a matter of staying awake but staying alert.

We didn't know as we stood in the pit area in support of United's £250,000 supercar carrying the club badge emblazoned on its bonnet what drama, disaster, despair and finally relief lay ahead of us. Geordies do nought by half and this had it all.

The headline on my exclusive report of February 5, 1996 splashed across page one of the *Chronicle* was stark in its message. "United car in crash terror" it boomed in what looked like six-foot-high letters. A subhead added: "Amazing escape as Magpie driver survives 190mph US track crash."

United's pride and joy had disintegrated after a spectacular crash going into a chicane. A Porsche clipped the Lister Storm, flipping it into the air before it broke into dozens of pieces.

Normally back-up teams take time off slipping back to their hotel for a quick meal before returning track side. However we were there when the black and white stripes of a Magpie took flight. The sickening feeling in the pit of my stomach almost doubled me up. Time stood still as the car twisted and turned in mid-air. Everyone was thinking the same yet everyone was silent.

Unbelievably, thankfully, the driver Ken Acheson was able to crawl out and walk away from the smouldering wreckage.

A 38-year-old ex-Formula One driver from Northern Ireland, Acheson was rushed to a local hospital in Daytona Beach with suspected whiplash injuries and concussion while the car was towed round to where we stood at United's garage. It was a mass of mangled metal minus bonnet, back and rear offside wheels. Thankfully a few hours later I was able to interview Ken, a married man with two children.

"I'm so happy to be alive," he told me. "However this is motor racing it's a dangerous sport and you have to accept that or get out."

There was to be no fairytale win for United (as so often the case) but was there ever so much dripping drama unfolding before tired eyes? This was a Beach party with a difference!

XXXXX

DENNIS WATERMAN may be an actor who strode both sides of the law in *The Sweeney* and *Minder* before gaining longevity with *New Tricks*.

However Waterman has very much a sporting background – he used to train as an amateur boxer in a London gym and his brother Peter became British and welterweight champion before tragedy struck, claiming him way ahead of his time.

Up here we remember Dennis, too, playing Bob Jones,

captain of the West Auckland team that won the first World Cup back in 1909, defeating the might of Juventus and successfully defended it two years later.

A Captain's Tale was a true story made in 1982 and Waterman, who participated in many charity football matches, was in his element as the crop haired leader of a bunch of miners who took the soccer world by storm.

While my first love has always been Newcastle United, Waterman knew of my passion for boxing and that fitted perfectly into his make-up. He told me of how his dad was a keen amateur boxer and how, aged 10, he himself began sparing at Caius Boxing Club. He was rated a good prospect. However Peter was something else.

"A dark haired Paul Newman, the most magnificent person I ever knew with unbelievable talent," said a proud brother.

Peter Waterman was the youngest boxer to represent Britain at the 1952 Helsinki Olympics and as a pro won the British and European welter titles.

He twice fought the legendary Kid Gavilan but in his 49th pro bout tragedy struck. Peter was pummelled to defeat by Dave Charnley and rushed to hospital where he was diagnosed with serious brain damage. At 21 years of age he would never be the same again. By 52 he was dead from a massive heart attack. Dennis was crushed.

Acting saved Dennis from a career risking life and limb like Peter but his love of the sport never waned. In the credits of *Minder*, you may recall, was a shot of Waterman in boxing shorts and gloves, his arms raised in victory.

XXXXX

GEOFF BOYCOTT and Brian Clough were like twins.

Both outrageously blunt, able to easily offend, and extremely opinionated. Both hugely successful in their respective sports. And, perhaps inevitably, close friends.

I shared a stage with both Boycott and Cloughie at talk-ins across the North East – separately of course – and they could certainly pull in and work a crowd.

Geoff is a Yorkshire man who knows the value of brass and it was hard going negotiating a financial deal with him but, my, once on stage he was full value. His knowledge of cricket is encyclopaedic and he would stay as long as people wanted. Playing and talking cricket was his life.

The Boycs I knew was a very private man. He was in a long-term relationship but worked very hard at keeping it out of the public eye. However I met and knew Anne Wyatt, a woman he met in 1958 when only 18 and she was 32 and they both worked at the Ministry Of Pensions in Barnsley.

For 20 years they lived in the village of Woolley, near Wakefield in West Yorkshire. However they eventually split up and Anne died from lung cancer at the age of 82 in 2009.

Boycott later married the woman who nursed him through his throat cancer. They have a daughter Emma.

I also worked with another controversial England star Ian Botham. When Sir Beefy joined Durham shortly after their elevation to first class cricket I ghosted his weekly column.

Like Boycott ever the opinionated, we were once reported to Lord's for a particular piece we did together.

Frisked for guns at world title fight

WHAT unbelieving eyes witnessed was like a throwback to Al Capone's *Chicago* **of the twenties when the mobster ruled a lawless city through terror and extortion.**

Russia had just thrown off its cloak of communism and cash now being king meant an open invite for gangsters and chancers to flood the big cities eager for easy pickings.

Moscow was to celebrate its 'liberation' in July of 1993 by staging its first ever professional boxing world title fight, with one-time IBF cruiserweight champion Glenn McCrory from our parts attempting to recapture his crown against American Alfred Cole.

I was one of the only hacks on the trip along with a TV crew when we flew into a grey, rain-lashed lawless capital.

All those Russians with ambitions to make a bundle had in the old days gone off to places like Miami in search of an illegal dollar, but the opening of a cash cow had them piling back into Moscow.

Boxing was an obvious attraction – it had been so on America's south coast for hard men of the Iron Curtain of course – and very quickly a piece of ominous muscle from Chechnya announced his arrival in our hotel.

He inevitably spoke with an American accent after his self imposed exile and told us "just call me Albert", which we did without question!

Albert insisted upon taking us who were part of the McCrory entourage round the city while our boy was tucked up in bed. Better to say yes and be safe than no and face possible danger.

Brother did he carry some clout. As a bodyguard he was better than Kevin Costner.

One night upon entering a heaving nightspot where obviously he was viewed with a mixture of awe and trepidation, he wanted us to have the best table in the house. So he simply walked down the front, lifted the steak plates of some unfortunates, and carried them to the back of the room where they were sat behind a pillar. Meanwhile he took centre stage and waved for us to join him!

Even Glenn witnessed the Wild East (as opposed to the Wild West) when he arrived at the plush Cherry Casino in downtown Moscow for the official weigh-in.

A burly bouncer who looked as though someone had chopped sticks on his face demanded to know if McCrory was carrying a gun and, if so, would he deposit it at the door before going through the metal detectors we associate with an airport today.

Glenn's brother Gary, manager Dave Gregory, and cuts man Dean Powell were similarly asked if they were carrying. On a table next to the screening I could see a pile of firearms, some in their holsters. Honest, I was looking round for Wyatt Earp and Doc Holliday!

"Aye, it was quite a trip what with Albert and me, a poor boxer, being asked to get rid of my gun before I stepped on the scales," smiled a shocked Glenn. "What did they think I was going to do? Shoot Al Cole?"

The fight itself took place in the CSKA Sports Palace where fans paid 5000 roubles or 500 dollars for a ringside seat to witness history in the making.

As with all world title fights TV is king and we were forced to wait until it was 'Midnight in Moscow' for the action to start so the bout could be beamed out live.

It lasted 12 torturous rounds with McCrory, showing the heart of a lion, twice hauling himself off the canvas in the sixth to go the distance. He never fought again.

I prefer to remember Glenn becoming the North East's first global champion on an epic night in Stanley when he destroyed the hopes of Patrick Lumumba and his 11th round knockout of Siza Makhathini in a Middlesbrough tent before the crippling cruiserweight restrictions made his task unsustainable, but playing Russian roulette in Moscow was an experience apart.

XXXXX

HERE where working class folk cherish local heroes we have produced many a fine athlete.

From Jim Alder to Charlie Spedding, Brendan Foster to Mike McLeod, Steve Cram to Jonathan Edwards. All men of true grit who have done us proud. Medal winners over and over again.

It has been my privilege to know them all and enjoy some special moments with them. Crammie became a good mate after I presented him with an award for setting a world record as a 17-year-old in the famed Emsley Carr mile. I knew his mam and dad, attended his wedding, and enjoyed a couple of sherbets on many an occasion.

For a while Cram and Edwards were untouchable in their respective events.

I was in Sydney (2000) when at last Jonathan hopped, stepped and jumped to his Olympic gold medal and amid obvious celebrations in the tunnel immediately afterwards, with the Union Jack draped round his shoulders, he made a point of finding me amongst the assembled jostling throng to make certain I got my quotes for back home.

A devout Christian, much later I sat with him in a Jesmond coffee house early one morning in between his commitments as a television commentator and he bravely admitted to becoming a non believer. A truly monumental step for a man like him to take.

With Big Bren we talked for many an hour about our joint love of Newcastle United and it's been an absolute pleasure to watch how he created and sustained the Great North Run, which stands as a monument to his all round organisational ability and vision.

However we had first seen that rare talent for making things happen when he opened and filled Gateshead's International Stadium with every world class athlete of his era.

The beautifully elegant Florence Griffith Joyner, Flo Jo herself with long finger nails and legs, the unbeatable Ed Moses, Olympic champ John Walker who was later struck down by Parkinson's Disease, the mystical Lasse Viren et al.

Foster's local rival Mike McLeod was tough of the track, a fine performer on track, road, and even country. He won an Olympic bronze AND silver medal in one race and ought to have had gold. That takes some doing, doesn't it?

It came about in Los Angeles 1984 in the 10,000 metres, a relentless slog that was heaven made for McLeod.

Mike magnificently achieved the bronze medal position when breasting the tape but the two in front of him were dodgy geezers.

Finn Martti Vainio, who finished second, was eventually stripped of his gong after a failed drugs test and McLeod was kicked up a place. However race winner Alberto Cova was later tainted by his involvement in a blood-boosting programme administered by the Italian track and field federation, which means Mike was the only clean finisher of the lot.

The consolation for him was that when silver was eventually hung round his neck prior to the start of the 1985 AAA Championship 10k in Battersea Park our Geordie boy conveniently forgot to take back his bronze gong.

I've always loved McLeod, a down to earth working lad whose feet always stayed on terra firma. When we still bump into one another it's an absolute joy.

Munich Massacre

MEMORIES are usually tinged with a warm glow, much amusement, or pride in a great achievement.

However occasionally it is absolute terror and the brutal loss of life that burns into your very soul.

More than 40 years ago I was at the epicentre of one of the worst atrocities ever committed in the name of sport.

The Munich Olympics were meant to be a showcase of athletic supremacy but instead they were plunged into the depths of hell when on September 5, 1972 Black September terrorists broke into the competitors village under the cloak of darkness to take hostage and finally slaughter 11 of the Israeli Olympic squad.

The atrocities took place over 20 long hours, extending from the Olympic Village to Furstenfeldbruck Airport.

Maybe it was dramatic, fascinatingly repulsive on live television, but I was there on the ground watching with unbelieving eyes amid the sobbing athletes who gathered within a stone's throw of the Israeli headquarters fearing for the lives of their comrades. You had to be part of it to feel the cutting tension and be gripped by terrible fear. To realise that evil had taken over the global playground. That sport which was supposed to unite nations was being raped by those who sought gain through violence.

I had arrived on German soil as a sportswriter but for a day I was a war correspondent and didn't know how I would ever be able to get back to the sheer joy of watching a human being make a 100 metres dash or hurl an iron ball as far as possible from a circle or see how high anyone could jump over the stick.

I didn't sleep for the 20 long, agonising hours it took for the hijack to reach its brutal conclusion. I dashed between the village and our Press centre, up a flight of stairs that seemed to get steeper by the hour, to relay the grimmest of news on an open telephone line back home.

Eight hooded terrorists from Black September, a Palestinian group with a hatred of Israel, were bent on bloodshed as they clambered over the wire fence which enclosed the men's village just before dawn on the 11th day of the Games of the XXth Olympiad. Carrying assault rifles and grenades, the Palestinians ran towards No. 31 Connollystrasse, the building housing the Israeli delegation.

Bursting into the first apartment they took a group of Israeli officials and trainers hostage. In another they captured the Israeli wrestlers and weightlifters. When the Israelis dared to fight back the Palestinians opened fire instantly, killing two. Another nine were subdued and taken hostage.

Black September demanded the release of 234 prisoners held in Israeli jails and the stand-off was under way.

I vividly recall a hastily summoned Press conference. Mark Spitz had become the greatest Olympian of all time, claiming seven gold medals and seven world records in swimming. I had been poolside looking on in astonishment every day of his triumphs.

However Spitz was an American Jew and he, like other Jews fearing more hostage-taking, was to flee back home.

Before he went Spitz spoke to the world's Press. At least I was told it was him. We could hear the words but couldn't see the man behind the bodyguards encircling the most famous sportsman on the planet.

The ruthless assault and the nature of the Israeli response thrust the Israeli-Palestinian crisis into the world spotlight, set the tone for decades of conflict in the Middle East and launched a new era of international terrorism.

Olympic events were suspended and broadcasters filled the time by switching to live footage from Connollystrasse. A TV audience of 900 million viewers in more than 100 countries watched with lurid fascination. Issa, the Black September leader, eventually wearied of negotiations and during the evening demanded a plane to fly his men and the Israelis to the Middle East.

German officials agreed to move the group in helicopters to Furstenfeldbruck airfield base on the outskirts of Munich where they said a Boeing 727 would be waiting to fly them to Cairo. Secretly, however, the Germans began planning a daring rescue operation at the airfield.

Just as the Palestinians and Israelis were about to arrive at Furstenfeldbruck a group of German policemen on the 727 took the fateful decision and abandoned their positions. Five German snipers were left to tackle eight well armed Palestinians. The hostages and terrorists arrived at the airfield at 10.40pm. Issa quickly realised it was a trap and the German snipers opening fire missing their targets. A gunfight erupted and bullets sliced through the control tower.

Myself and a group of journos caught up in the drama had decided to give chase in a taxi, stupidly, hopelessly, swept along by sheer adrenaline. We could hear the gunfire ahead of us echoing in the pitch darkness. Reality set in. This was no place to play hero.

An hour of sporadic gunfire ended when German armoured cars trundled onto the airfield. The gunner in one car accidentally shot a couple of men on his own side and the Palestinians apparently thought they were about to be machine gunned. A terrorist shot four of the hostages in one helicopter as another Black September guerrilla tossed a grenade inside. The explosion ignited the fuel tank and the captive Israelis burned. Eleven Israelis, five Palestinians, and one German police officer perished during what became known as the Munich Massacre.

I recall sitting in the splendid Munich stadium as the Olympics restarted and wondering what I was doing. All sport seemed so futile. I watched with a heavy heart.

To be frank I didn't feel I wanted the Olympics to continue but quickly I realised they must. Terror must never be allowed to win.

XXXXX

ARTHUR McKENZIE is a man of considerable talents who

has enjoyed three separate careers. First as an international athlete, second a copper on the streets of Newcastle and third a renowned and super successful TV scriptwriter with credits for *The Bill*, *Wycliffe*, *Casualty* and the like.

I've known him throughout and still pop round to Arthur's house in Gosforth for a cup of char and a chinwag while his lovely lady supplies us with biccies.

Naturally bearing in mind he excelled as a discus and shotputter, as well as a copper, he is a giant of a man with the perfect background for becoming a writer on life.

He was good enough to finish fourth, just out of the medals, in the 1970 Commonwealth Games and tells some hilarious tales about his time when international athletics and a boy in blue overlapped.

Once when winding up in the throwing net at London's White City, a rascal whose collar he was trying to feel yelled from the crowd: "I'm over here Arthur!" Enough to put you off your stride I would think!

McKenzie spent 31 years as a detective inspector in charge of the toughest division of Newcastle's west end and investigated corruption in Hong Kong – of which there was plenty.

During his career he was commended on 27 occasions for exemplary police work ranging from national drugs busts, disarming mentally deranged persons, to clearing up major crime.

As I've said, that gave him plenty of background material when he took up pen instead of truncheon. He wrote 24 episodes of *The Bill* in just 18 months. His latest film to hit the cinemas is *Harrigan* starring the ever so popular Stephen

Tompkinson. I was privileged to be one of Arthur's guests at the red carpet opening of his gritty cop story, set naturally in his native North East, as was another local athlete Jim Alder, whose life story was ghosted by his mate.

The two of them are still real value for money.

A drunken champ with a loaded gun

WE WERE confronted by a skyscraper of a man naked apart from a pink towel bound tightly round his waist.

It was 10 o'clock in the morning but our host had already been swigging a bottle of rum and had a cigarette dangling from his lips Robert Mitchum style. More chilling still, he was waving a gun around.

I had travelled with my best mate Glenn McCrory to Havana, capital of Cuba, to meet boxing legend Teofilo Stevenson, a three-time Olympic gold medal winner.

A man who took the Olympics of Munich '72, Montreal '76, and Moscow '80 by storm.

Such was his standing within Cuba that their grateful leader Fidel Castro had given Stevenson his home free of charge…and that ruddy gun which was now getting more than an airing.

We went through to his back garden where the swimming pool was empty apart from wisps of weeds. The dustbin, though, was full to overflowing with discarded empty bottles of rum.

Stevenson was loaded – but what we didn't know was that the gun was too! Not until he playfully took a pot shot at something that caught his eye in his neighbour's garden.

Now a drunken ex-fighting man with a gun full of bullets added up to big danger. We wanted out.

When McCrory suggested a photo to divert attention from his weapon Stevenson, still a proud warrior in his declining years, disappeared into his bedroom to put on his Cuba tracksuit and dumped his ciggie in an ashtray.

His public image worldwide had to be maintained, though the gun was tucked inside the waistband of his trousers hidden out of sight. Afterwards Stevenson insisted in his broken English that he stayed with us for the rest of the day and we gingerly ordered a taxi to take us into the heart of Havana, where Teofilo wanted to meet some of his mates in a bar. Ominously that meant more drinking.

Upon arrival we were ushered upstairs where Stevenson, a beloved figure to his people, was quickly surrounded by those who came to bask in reflected glory.

Glenn and I looked at one another and nodded. It was time to go – and quickly.

We slid away unnoticed and, once outside, took to our toes. I swear we would have taken Usain Bolt to the tape!

Bottom of the road, a taxi hailed, and we breathed a massive sigh of relief. A gun-toting former Olympic champion had scared us as much as when he struck terror into the hearts of his opponents in his pomp.

Stevenson's house was no palace. Not only was the

swimming pool unused and a magnet for weeds but a couple of panels of glass were missing from the back door, there was no air conditioning in the small rooms to combat stifling heat and framed photos of his illustrious career took over half a wall, hiding cracks.

One was of Teofilo with Muhammad Ali, another of Castro in military combats raising the gloved hand of a young and handsome world champion with a "Happy 50th birthday" message from his leader.

In 2012, still only 60 years of age, Teofilo Stevenson died of a heart attack probably hastened by his love of rum and ciggies. When I heard the news I felt overwhelming sadness.

XXXXX

AS A kid I was an avid autograph collector with some decent back up – I knew literary agent Thea Benson through my auntie and through her Ivy Crane Wilson, who wrote the famous Hollywood Albums over in America.

I have a cracking collection – Marilyn Monroe whose signature is extra special because she signed herself Marilyn Monroe Miller during her marriage to the playwright Arthur Miller; Humphrey Bogart who bewitched me enough that years later I made a pilgrimage to Casablanca with Glenn McCrory to visit a bar in honour of his epic film; plus the likes of Tyrone Power, Peter Sellars, Brigitte Bardot, Sirs Alec Guinness and Dirk Bogarde, Jack Lemmon, Laurence Harvey, Eartha Kitt, Johnnie Ray, Joan Crawford, Rod Steiger, Diana Dors, Deborah Kerr, Van Johnson and Cyd Charisse.

Naturally I possess the scribbled writings of a fair few sporting icons too – Emile Zatopek, Archie Moore, Sir Stanley Matthews, Len Hutton, Cliff Morgan, Denis Compton, John Charles, Frank Tyson, Ezzard Charles, Randy Turpin, Bert Trautmann, Frank Worrell and the full Newcastle United FA Cup winning side of 1951 sitting proudly behind the silver pot.

When I worked as a hack in Fleet Street between two spells with the *Chron* I ghosted the autobiographies of West Indies Test stars Wes Hall and Rohan Kanhai and, through them, got to know a young cricketer called Basil D'Oliveira who had left his native South Africa when forced out by apartheid and signed for Worcester the year before.

I exchanged several letters and enjoyed several meetings with Dolly and actually have a contract to this day signed by him and dated April 26, 1965 sent to my Worple Road address in Raynes Park agreeing that I should write his book.

Of course it would be hugely controversial, especially at the time given his background, and the Worcester committee, taking in water, blocked it. Three years later the D'Oliveira Affair exploded upon the world when England picked him for a proposed tour to South Africa, whose apartheid government immediately refused his entry. The tour was off and the letters, I feel, form part of that explosive time.

However despite such a passionate love of all sport I have as an adult only ever asked one person for their autograph and that was Muhammad Ali. It came about when Ali toured Tyneside with his new bride, an event I covered of course, and The Greatest appeared at the Eldon Square Recreation Centre on Saturday, July 16, 1977.

A one and a half hour show kicked off at 3pm and was screened live on World Of Sport (Reg Gutteridge was the compere).

I was backstage with Ali. He wasn't in fine fettle – indeed he was under the weather – but he signed his book *The Greatest* with a heavy, deliberate hand which made an indent for page upon page.

Once in front of the cameras, however, Ali came to life and was the wise-cracking, singing and dancing man the world knew and loved.

Souness conned

FORMER Newcastle manager Graeme Souness was the victim of the biggest con in British football.

And I was the chairman who dared sign Ali Dia immediately after Souness was duped!

Yep, it was like having a front row seat at a Mr Bean convention.

The year was 1996 and Souness was in charge of Southampton when he received a mysterious phone call from a man purporting to be the one-time FIFA World Player of the Year George Weah, a footballing superstar.

'George' told a gullible and excited Souness that he might like to cast his gaze over his cousin, a Paris St Germain striker who had won international caps with Senegal.

In the days before YouTube, where a routine spot check is enough to tell someone all they need to know about a potential purchase, a personal recommendation from one of the game's greats was enough to make Souness go all gooey.

He didn't want to lose out on a gem lobbed into his lap

by accident and therefore, instead of offering Dia a trial, he dived in to tie him down on a one-month contract.

Time enough for the new Matt le Tissier to prove his Weah credentials in the Premier League.

Unfortunately for Souness and Southampton the phone call was a great big fake. The suggestion was it came from Dia himself, or at least one of his pals.

Ali had never played for Senegal, wasn't on the books of PSG, wasn't George Weah's cousin, and had only turned out for a few unheard-of French clubs plus one in Germany.

So the fact that Dia pulled on a Southampton shirt during a Premier League game against Leeds United must rank as one of the most bizarre happenings the game has ever witnessed and be a lasting embarrassment to a former European Cup winner, the man who picked him.

Saints legend Le Tissier revealed that Dia trained only once with the first team squad, showing as much Premier League skill in a five-a-side game as a guy with his feet tied together.

Not one member of the Southampton team thought Dia would ever be involved in a matchday squad. Imagine their surprise, then, when Souness named his new Senegalese international on the bench for a crunch match with Leeds. After Le Tissier pulled a thigh muscle during the game, the number 33 went up on the fourth official's board, signalling that Dia would be introduced for his debut. One superstar off, one on!

What happened next was excruciatingly embarrassing for everyone who witnessed it. Dia ran around like Bambi on ice and a short while later the substitute was substituted as

Souness realised his terrible, terrible mistake, hauling Dia off to be replaced by Ken Monkou.

Leeds won the game 2-0 and the most ambiguous of Premier League matches passed into folklore. The tale of the Saint who became a sinner was regaled in pubs up and down the country.

Dia never showed up at The Dell again. Indeed he did a moonlight flit from his hotel on the south coast and ended up in my office at Gateshead's International Stadium.

How? Well, I knew Ali's agent Peter Harrison, a Geordie who had once played central defence alongside Philippe Albert in Belgium.

Peter was taking Dia over to Carlisle United for a trial but popped in to see me with Souness's tormentor in tow.

Now Gateshead weren't Southampton. They didn't play in the Premier League but the Football Conference which was a very different standard of course. Maybe Dia couldn't hack it at the club which had once housed a centre-forward called Alan Shearer but that was not to say he couldn't successfully play part-time football. Ali was quick – lightning quick – and we needed a striker.

I spoke with my manager and a couple of other director's then, deciding no one could take Dia at his word, I phoned the police on the south coast and the hotel where our intrepid international footballer had hung his hat. There had been a whisper Ali had ran over an unfortunate chambermaid coming up the drive when making his quick getaway in his car and that his bill had remained unpaid.

Anyway we got all that sorted and decided that on a match to match basis we couldn't lose in signing Mr Dia.

In fact he scored on his Gateshead debut against Bath City and in all made eight appearances for us netting twice before our new manager Jim Platt, the former Middlesbrough and Northern Ireland goalkeeper, did a Souness and subbed the sub when Dia got on in a game at Welling.

Ali went on to play a few matches with Blyth Spartans and enrolled at Northumbria University to study business before he fell off the radar. However there was one final twist in the tale of Ali Dia.

A little while later former Newcastle United striker Alan Shoulder, who had become my reserve-team manager, walked into the office after training one night.

He told me a guy had come up to him in the car park and asked if he could join in training with a view to playing for us. Nothing too unusual about that.

"What's his name?" I asked.

Shoulder rummaged in his tracksuit pocket and pulled out a piece of paper.

Looking at it he replied: "Ali Dia."

XXXXX

TALKING of scallywags, we had another in charge of Darlington's football club.

George Reynolds is a one-time safe blower who has done porridge twice after having his collar felt.

I got to know George well – he was chairman of Darlo at a time when I was the chair at Gateshead and besides I was a hack and George was ruddy good copy. He loved the limelight too. Hence our coming together.

A flamboyant character who wore a combover hairstyle with pins in it for safety, he regularly boasted of cracking safes and in describing his takeover of Darlington would say with much pomp and pause for effect: "As a kid I was sold into slavery suffering beatings, hunger, misery and fear; then branded illiterate, mentally deficient and backward. All the ingredients were there to become chairman of a football club."

Actually his background was pretty much like that.

The stories used to come pouring forth – how he got his wife Susan to read out a prepared statement at a fans forum he had called in which she announced: "It's not unknown for games to be thrown." The only trouble was all the Darlo players were sitting there. They walked out!

Later Reynolds told me with obvious glee how he bugged the home dressing room and would listen to what players said about him. Boy, was he thick-skinned!

Another of his stunts was trying to sign Newcastle's old flamboyant striker Tino Asprilla, only this time George had met his match.

Reynolds got as far as presenting Tino to the crowd before a home match with Carlisle United. Asprilla was photographed walking round the ground shaking the hands of delirious fans with Georgie boy, wearing his broadest of smiles, never far out of camera shot.

Only trouble was at five o'clock on the morning Tino was due to have his medical he did a runner.

He was picked up by friends living in Newcastle and taken to the city's airport where he caught a flight to Gatwick for another flight on to the Middle East. While he had been talking to Darlington, Tino had also been in negotiations with an Arab club.

It was George of course who built Darlo a 25,000 all-seater stadium, not unexpectedly to be called the George Reynolds Stadium in his honour, and told me with total conviction how he would nick 8,000 fans apiece from Newcastle United, Sunderland and Middlesbrough and parachute the club into the Premier League.

The traditional way of running a football club was not for him. It wasn't his style. Cutting corners, being confrontational, and extremely colourful. That was the cut of his jib.

After his second prison stint I went round to his new apartment with radio presenter Paul Gough for a gargle and a catch-up. He had reinvented himself as an after-dinner speaker with Goffy his agent and was as outrageous as ever.

Safe blower, jailbird, millionaire businessman and genial dinner host. George Reynolds was all things to all men.

Nightclub boss who became top talent spotter

A FLAMBOYANT Geordie who used to rejoice in pink jackets and long flowing locks, Monty ran a floating nightclub which inevitably meant rubbing shoulders with pop stars and footballers.

It was a life touched by glamour and filled with bucketloads of babes, but even more by bleary-eyed late nights and beer-filled youths feeling their strength.

Yet amazingly Paul Montgomery emerged from the smoky atmosphere of swinging nightlife to become an ace football scout who has been responsible for unearthing and signing talent worth literally a king's ransom. What were the odds on that?

In my nightclubbing days Monty was simply the guy who ran the Tuxedo Princess moored on the Gateshead bank of the Tyne. A big extrovert, a good pal and, yes, football mad. But then aren't most Geordies?

Little did I realise that the Montgomery who entertained a bevy of footballers on Michael Quadrini's floating nightclub would become a key scout for our club Newcastle United, working with managers such as Sir Bobby Robson, Jim Smith, Glenn Roeder and Sam Allardyce.

From Pavel Srnicek to Olivier Bernard, he helped new arrivals land at St James' Park.

It had all began with the Bald Eagle's visits to the Tux. Jim loved a night out, loved a pint and a cigar, and we would all chew the fat propping up the bar rather than dancing the light fantastic.

Obviously Monty impressed Smith during our football fuelled talks because he asked him to do a bit of scouting and a new career was born.

Monty helped blow away the myth that to recognise raw footballing ability you must have been a top footballer yourself.

Jack Hixon worked for British Rail yet discovered Alan Shearer and a barrowload of gilt-edged kids while Monty was a nightclub manager who operated above the schoolboy level where Hixon excelled to bring forth the brightest of already existing talent.

Yet Monty never played above local football level in his native North West Durham and managed no one other than his own highly successful Sunday morning team.

A Northern League player at 16 who, while attending Durham University, 'starred' for Bede College alongside two distinguished team-mates – future Carlisle chairman Michael Knighton and David Parnaby, who did so much to shape Middlesbrough's famed academy.

However injury effectively finished Paul's career at 19.

Such was the sound eye Monty had for burgeoning talent

that Jim Smith employed him for 10 years at three different clubs including Newcastle.

Sir Bobby, too, paid ready lip service to a guy he called his "rough diamond."

To work for United on so many separate occasions was a dream for Monty, who always maintained in moments of quiet reflection over a chilled wine that "I was brought up not to eat bacon because it's red and white."

Montgomery worked with former United skipper Glenn Roeder at both Newcastle and West Ham.

Indeed Monty had been at his side on the day Roeder was struck down by a brain tumour at only 47 years of age and rushed to hospital to undergo emergency surgery.

He told me later: "It was absolutely dreadful. I had been to France on a scouting mission and came back to Upton Park for our match with Middlesbrough.

"I sat behind Glenn in our dug-out and, yes, the situation was tense because we were in the middle of a big relegation battle. But we won the game and afterwards in the dressing-room Glenn told me to pop into his office as he had some food coming.

"However, it was a Bank Holiday Monday and I didn't know the times of the trains to Newcastle and so I said no, I'd better get away.

"I was on the train north when I got a call on my mobile telling me what had happened to Glenn. It was horrible. Honestly, if I'd been there I would have collapsed with him. It certainly put life into perspective." After fighting to regain his fitness Roeder was very quickly sacked by West Ham.

"No-one deserves what happened to him, whether or not

you are a football manager and your team is in danger of going down," maintained his Geordie friend.

"I was watching a match on TV on a Sunday afternoon when it suddenly came across the bottom of the screen that Roeder had been sacked. That's how I found out his fate."

Inevitably Monty and Roeder first became friends when Glenn was the highly-popular skipper of Newcastle in the early 80s and Paul was running a city nightclub.

"He used to come into the club and babysit Paul Gascoigne," laughed Montgomery. "I'd get phone calls from Glenn saying: 'What's the little b******d up to?'"

"Actually Gazza loved Glenn. He was a father figure to him and kept him right. Roeder almost went with him to Rome when Gazza signed for Lazio to act as minder but he had his own career to consider."

XXXXX

MY JOB down the years has been to know what is going on in this sports mad city of ours.

Yet when I had one of my best nights ever I hadn't the faintest idea of what was happening behind my back.

In March of 2005 I was awarded the Wilkinson Sword for services to sport at the black tie Sport Newcastle annual dinner in the splendid surrounds of the Civic Centre.

Now part of the deal usually is that secretary Malcolm Dix fills me in with a list of the top award winners prior to the dinner so that I can prepare my story for the *Chron*. Of course I'm sworn to secrecy. Those to be happily surprised must have no idea.

So I got my list for Sports Personality of the Year etc and next to Wilkinson Sword was the name of Steve Black, the motivating coach of Newcastle Falcons.

Steve is a close pal of mine which meant I had to be very careful at the VIP pre-dinner drinks session not to inadvertently mention his good fortune.

I must admit Blackie looked a little smug but Gibbo said nowt. I could keep a secret. He would understand.

When the build-up came to announcing the Wilkinson Sword winner it struck me immediately that it didn't sound like Blackie's CV. Then there was talk of working in Hexham, very shortly afterwards about owning a football club. Gawd, it was me!

Normally I talk for England. Everybody says so. However when I walked up to the top table I was literally shaking from the surprise of it all and when asked straight bat and pad questions by my Beeb buddy Jeff Brown, all I could do was mumble something about hoping Newcastle United won a trophy in my lifetime. What a wit!!

As I walked away with a sword big enough to slay a dragon my editor on the top table gave me a wink. Was everybody in on it bar yours truly? I still count the Wilkinson Sword as my most treasured award, made that much better by the names around it. The previous winner was Jonathan Edwards and the next after me Alan Shearer.

Others to be so honoured by getting a hernia picking up a shining blade include Sir Bobby Robson, Jackie Milburn, Jack Charlton, Brendan Foster, Sir John Hall and Joe Harvey.

To be a little geezer amongst such Geordie giants I take as quite something.

Forgotten hero I found in a Georgia graveyard

HISTORY sometimes buries legends beneath the heavy weight of time.

A hundred years or so is a long memory challenge and so a Geordie who literally changed the face of golf had been largely forgotten in his native land. Until a chance exchange of words on home territory triggered action.

Michael Newrick was the grandson of J Douglas Edgar, as colourful as a kaleidoscope, as charismatic as a movie heart throb and a womaniser par excellence.

Little did I think that a chance meeting in a small bungalow tucked away within a Gosforth estate would lead me to Edgar's grave on a sun scorched hill in an Atlanta cemetery and the creation of an annual golf tournament held in his name and honour.

It all began simply enough. A friend of mine had worked with Michael when teenagers and they bumped into one another. Grandad was mentioned, I was told of it, and a meet was arranged.

Newrick, living alone and confined in the main to a wheelchair, was rightfully proud of the superb golfer and teacher who left for America in search of fame and fortune. Prior to our get together Michael had visited the bank vault that housed much memorabilia to bring it forth and capture my attention.

Before me were the ancient golf clubs that took Edgar to victories in the French and Canadian Opens, private letters penned by husband to wife, and other such personal effects piled high on the floor.

The story I was told was like a flight of fancy. A young man from working class stock, a scallywag who loved women, drink and gambling in equal measure, invented the modern golf swing no less to revolutionise the sport, and set off across the pond determined to become a pro on the lucrative American circuit.

He did, too, teaching legends and winning tournaments in equal measure, but his extra-marital dalliances brought disaster and death amid controversy and dripping drama.

Before I left Michael Newrick's house I had promised to tell J Douglas Edgar's story and to do something further to rejuvenate his reputation at home. I didn't quite know what but I intended to talk to Glenn McCrory, my partner when we made a series of sporting documentaries.

The outcome which naturally took time eventually saw us fly the Atlantic in search of the truth and to claim a magnificent trophy from Edgar's old club Druid Hills to be played for annually on the golf courses of Tyneside.

That's how Glenn and I came to find ourselves standing at the intersection of Fifth and West Peachtree in midtown

Atlanta, Georgia where almost a century ago a Geordie golf champion lay bloodied and dying in the road.

Edgar's life had been snuffed out 4,000 miles from home and the world of golf had been robbed of one of its most stylish exponents.

He was mowed down in a hit and run on the very corner where we stood with our minds drifting back to what must have occurred that fateful warm August night of 1921.

The charismatic Edgar was only 35 years of age when he died under the wheels of a car bloodied and alone. He had spent but two years at Druid Hills yet his achievements had been immense.

Was his death the result of an accident? Or was he murdered on the instructions of an Asian underworld figure because the little Geordie had a clandestine affair with the gangster's wife?

The case is officially still open after all this time, though general opinion tends to sway towards the dark hand of a murderer. Certainly his grandson bought into the sex and revenge theory.

We moved across town from the scene of Edgar's violent death to Westview Cemetery, where he was laid to rest on the other side of the globe from his wife and two children.

Edgar wasn't brought home. Instead his cherry casket draped with a huge Union Jack was dropped into the red clay of a foreign land.

Our Geordie's headstone, still standing to this very day, simply reads: "J Douglas Edgar, a native of England, one of the great golfers of the age." I doubt if he ever thought in his most fanciful moments that Geordie folk would fly from his home city to Georgia to stand at his grave and salute a man dead for nigh on a century.

Douglas had lived a colourful existence, a man who broke every single golf record as well as the rules of life itself, invented the modern swing, and coached such icons as Bobby Jones, a true son of Atlanta.

He had won the French Open and twice the Canadian Open in a career arrowed permanently towards golden success until it ended so abruptly.

Such was the widely felt sorrow at his passing that Frenchman Louis Tellier, a close friend of Edgar and a delightful golfer, committed suicide by hanging on his 35th birthday, the same age as Douglas when he died.

Hollywood would do well to record the story of our Geordie maverick. Sylvester Stallone's Rocky is fictional but this is even more outlandish, a heady mix of sex, booze, gambling and mobsters yet is 100 per cent reality.

Chad O'Dell is now the Druid Hills pro and was our host on a very nostalgic visit of discovery.

"We are fully aware of the debt we owe J Douglas," O'Dell told me. "He not only put Druid Hills on the map by winning the Canadian Open of 1919 with a: record score but promoted the city of Atlanta which at the time was viewed as monumental. Edgar may have been a Geordie proud of his roots but he was taken into the hearts of all Atlantans.

"His aggregate score of 278 at the Hamilton Golf and Country Club was a record for a major event which stood for 17 years but it was the margin of Edgar's victory that was so startling.

"He won by 16 shots over his student Bobby Jones, Western Open winner Long Jim Barnes, and defending champion Karl Keffer. It was Bobby Jones' best finish to date in any national open yet the largest margin of defeat he had ever suffered.

"That 16-shot record still stands today as the largest margin of victory in a top flight event. Tiger Woods came close in 2000 with a 15-shot victory in the US Open at Pebble Beach but even he in his pomp couldn't top Edgar.

"A lot of people in Newcastle these days might not realise how great a golfer Douglas was but that fact alone ought to give them a good idea."

When I mentioned the more colourful side of Edgar's personality Chad smiled in recognition.

"I'll tell you a story that we actually included in our book on the history of Druid Hills which we published in 1997," he said. "Tommy Wilson had been Douglas's best friend in England – he had caddied for Edgar and was his assistant at the Northumberland Golf Club. Anyway Douglas persuaded Tommy to come over and be his assistant at our club.

"Edgar loved a drink but this was the time of prohibition which infuriated him.

"Of course he found ways round the ban like so many did and one night when the worse for wear he and Wilson walked into a car showroom in Atlanta where upon Douglas ordered two 8,500-dollar limousines, one for himself and one for his friend. That was colossal money in such days.

"When the two cars were delivered to him at the golf

club next day with a bill for 17,000 dollars the hungover Edgar had no recollection of ordering them.

"Wilson had to explain to a flustered salesman, 'We haven't got 17 dollars in the bank, never mind 17,000'.

"Douglas was like a child with money. He used to talk of making a million dollars on his golf book explaining how to play the game, but if he had done so three-quarters of it would have been spent before the cheque arrived."

Maybe Edgar had been largely forgotten with the passing of so many years, yet when we visited Westview Cemetery I was given a long list of notables buried on its 500-acre site and top of the list was our Geordie.

He is in grave three of plot 14 on a hill of burned grass just a golf chip away from where many of the Confederate soldiers from the Civil War are buried and honoured beneath a massive statue and a fluttering Confederate flag.

It is exactly 100 years since Edgar spectacularly won the French Open as World War One was about to engulf all in bloody conflict. Appropriately in celebration of what occurred a century ago, the J Douglas Edgar Trophy established by McCrory and myself is now on annual offer on gold days around the region.

My only regret is that Michael Newrick never lived to see our promise to him reach fruition. He died suddenly and unexpectedly at his Gosforth home.

Small men, big hearts

OFTEN there is a mighty big heart inside the wee frame of a man. It allows him to stage a brave and defiant fight against the sinking of the sun.

Terry Hibbitt and Jackie Sinclair waged such a war upon the deadliest of opponents: cancer. They may have been defeated in the end but, my, did they show courage and grit.

To lose them was a heartache. I knew both ever so well. They were from my time on the road twenty four seven with Newcastle United.

Indeed they both represent glorious times in black and white history. Hibby was the magician who set up goals for SuperMac and played in the 1974 FA Cup final while Sinclair was a European Fairs Cup winner five years earlier.

When little Jackie left us a short while back, on a cruise with his wife to enjoy some precious time together, he was 67. Still far too young to meet his maker.

However Terry was only 46 when he died in August of 1994. A man just touching middle age.

When he went into hospital for a second time to be told his cancer was terminal I spoke at some length with his wife Jennifer.

They were both 16 when they met at the Mecca dance hall in Leeds (admittance 20p). Five years later they were married.

Jennifer told heart-warming stories of a fiery little fighter's defiance of the inevitable.

He had a knockabout in a hospital corridor with a white-coated doctor who had walked into his room and announced: "I've always wanted to say I played football with Terry Hibbitt. Do you mind?" With that he produced a black and white plastic ball from behind the potted plants.

Terry was sent home of course once the unchangeable outcome was known. He had been bar manager at the Diamond pub in Ponteland, not a corner kick away from his Darras Hall home.

I call it the footballers' pub because so many have downed drink there down the years and, sure enough, the Saturday before he died Hibby popped in to have a beer with his pals.

Malcolm Macdonald used to say with a mischievous grin that Hibby "could cause an argument in an empty house." He was lippy, the wee man, but he was an artist when at work.

Joe Harvey walked into the Newcastle dressing room one day and announced to SuperMac: "I've just bought the man who will make your goals." It was Hibby from Leeds United.

Joe knew how to handle his stars. Each was an individual with differing needs and Harvey had them sussed. Where he would tell the super confident Macdonald that he was "a bandy-legged so and so who had better get his finger out" he would put a loving arm round Hibby and give him a fag!

Jackie Sinclair, who had returned to his hometown of Dollar in Scotland, stood a mere 5ft 6in but possessed the grit and determination of the mining community where he was brought up.

I broke the story of Jackie's fight against cancer several months before he died when he asked me to let Newcastle's fans, who had displayed such warmth towards him, know he had been handed a death penalty.

With great fortitude he insisted: "I don't want anyone to feel sorry for me. It's just I want Geordie people who have been so good to me to be with me in my fight."

"It was a hammer blow when I was first told I had cancer. I know what I'm facing, I know I'll probably lose the fight, but I want to fight the fight."

Jackie took his inspiration from his wife Lynne, who had successfully battled cancer for years, and was accompanied on virtually every visit to hospital by his close friend and fellow '69 team-mate Jim Scott.

The passing of time inevitably costs us heroes. Just as Terry Hibbitt became the first of the 1974 FA Cup final side to pass away, Jackie Sinclair was the first of the Fairs Cup legends.

xxxxx

HOWEVER you are involved in football, working inside a club is a whole new experience.

As a hack writing about the game I felt I ought to have

the bottle to try and run a club. Don't be all mouth and no substance. Anyway for my sins I ended up chairman and eventually owner of Gateshead for 11 years. That meant amongst many things working closely with the manager on signings. Now that is a real eye opener.

No names, no pack drill but I had one player who turned up at the International Stadium for talks with a rather buxom girlfriend in tow. After the initial introductions he turned to this dolly bird and said: "Show the chairman your t**s." We signed her instead of him (only kidding on that bit!).

Another player of real quality had a massive problem. He used to bet on three-legged horses.

Regular as clockwork he would come through from Middlesbrough where he lived and be standing outside the back door of the *Chronicle* waiting for me to emerge for a fag and then balefully put his case for the club helping to pay off a rather agitated bookie.

Then there was a former Football League striker who scored goals for fun. Because he realised his value to the team he asked if I would finance his vasectomy. Evidently his wife didn't want any more kids.

Less than a year later he was back knocking on my door. Would I pay for a reversal? He had parted from his wife and now had a young girlfriend who was keen on starting a family.

It's a snip being a chairman!

XXXXX

HAVING been a fan before a hack I have a tremendous

fascination with the No.9 legends of a historic club. Knowing this, when United historian Paul Joannou wrote a book called Shirt of Legends he asked me to pen the introduction and Alan Shearer to do the foreword. I've always liked to keep good company!

Centre-forwards are the glamour boys, they are who we hold dear. Dashing heroes scoring spine-tingling goals to slay the greatest of opposition.

Men we can see vividly just by closing our eyes.

Being in a privileged position I got to know three of the best very well: Wor Jackie, SuperMac and Big Al. I also rubbed shoulders with another two I place just behind our top trio, Wyn Davies and Len White.

Maybe they all had one thing in common, the ability to be classic attackers, but they were very different as men.

While Wor Jackie was shy and genuinely surprised at the public adulation he received, SuperMac walked with the arrogant strut of self confidence, always ready to run off at the mouth.

Shearer is somewhere in between. Having been a star since he was 17 and scored a hat-trick against Arsenal, he was groomed by his mentor Jack Hixon to say the right things in public. Be a political animal.

You have to earn Alan's trust and then never let him down but if you do that you discover the man beneath the surface. A loyal friend with a wicked sense of humour.

Shearer and Paul Gascoigne both came to my rescue when my club Gateshead got into financial difficulties through our main sponsor suddenly pulling out without warning mid season. Both starred in separate shows without asking for a penny in return when they could command very tasty pay nights.

I remember being in the Newcastle Press room after a match when the door burst open and in walked Alan still in his playing kit. He had come up the tunnel and instead of heading for the dressing-room turned sharp left.

Pulling off his sweat-stained No.9 top, he threw it at me and said: "Here, stick this in your auction." He had just scored a hat-trick!

Big Wyn Davies was different again. His public image was of an aloof guy with no time for the Press.

We used to kid that he would negotiate to buy a *Chron* rather than pay full whack and would buy bruised fruit in the Chester-le-Street market while waiting to be picked up by the team coach.

However in later years I've become close to the big fella. As the president of the Fairs Club which regularly brings United's old European winners to Tyneside, I've been thrown together with Davies.

We get on well, so well that Wyn actually apologised for being such a pain during his playing days. "I only wish I had relaxed more and enjoyed it," he told me.

Enjoy it now mate. It's not too late!

East Ender heart throb cut down

HE MAY have been manager of Sunderland, which to a Geordie means fraternising with the enemy, but Denis Smith was first and foremost a football man.

Denis was a bloke's bloke, a one time centre-half who ate timid forwards for breakfast washed down with a pint of paint stripper.

Anyway he was just passing through at Sunderland on a long and meandering career path.

I got to know a lot of Roker managers through the Hennessy lunches involving the North East's big three clubs we used to put on at a restaurant in Jesmond Dene, which lasted until the fading light gave out. Some, I stress some, became good pals. Like Smithy, Peter Reid who had a great repartee with United fans, Malcolm Crosby who did a bit of coaching for me at Gateshead, and Viv Busby who first became a social buddy when on loan at Newcastle during the infamous Hereford period.

A couple of red and white players also entered the Gibbo

inner circle through talk-ins I used to chair across our area featuring both a Newcastle and Sunderland star. The best from Mackem land were Marco Gabbiadini, Don Goodman and Kevin Ball. They took the baiting of a Geordie (me) in good spirit.

Anyway back to Denis Smith, who made his hardman reputation in the red and white stripes not of Sunderland but Stoke City, though he always stressed to me that he missed the FA Cup tie when Blyth Spartans went down to the Victoria Ground and gave them a walloping.

Buzzer (Viv Busby) didn't, he played. Come to think of it he had a terrible record in the infamous giant-killing matches of the day – not only was he in the Stoke side that lost to Spartans but he did of course play for Newcastle when they were sensationally put out by another non-league side Hereford United.

Smithy, like Reidie, strutted in his image of a man who stood no-nonsense and I remember him playing in a charity match at Gateshead's International Stadium.

A bunch of celebs, many from *Coronation Street* and *EastEnders*, were pitted against a side of ex-players of which Denis was the centre-half.

The real heart throb of the time was Nick Berry. Remember him? He was Simon Wicks in *EastEnders*, a fella who could send female hearts fluttering from 50 paces especially after releasing a No.1 single *Every Loser Wins*. Berry went on to star as PC Nick Rowan in *Heartbeat*.

The idea of these charity games is to entertain. As simple as that. Let there be many goals, let those who have attracted the crowd have their moment in the sun.

The attendance was good, there was a significant number of young ladies on hand given it was a football match played in the main by old fogies.

We knew why. When Nick Berry got the ball just over the halfway line and made progress the ooohs and aaahs were getting louder and louder.

Pop Robson let him go past without any sort of half hearted challenge. So did a couple of others.

By now our hero was approaching the edge of the penalty area. Out of the corner of my eye I saw this blurred figure eating ground. In one movement he launched himself and, two-footed, brought down Simon Wicks somewhere around his stocking tops. The ooohs gave way to gasps of horror and concern.

Smithy had struck. Even in a charity match he couldn't let anyone go unchallenged.

"Sorry Gibbo," he said with a shrug after the game, "but there was no way I was going to let that little bugger score!"

When I was chairman of Gateshead I always seemed to be running into Sunderland backroom staff. Perhaps that's why I wanted to win so badly! Take our FA Cup run in 2000. Having beaten Halifax Town away in the first round when they were a Football League club managed by Peter Reid's old assistant Paul Bracewell we were drawn at Swindon Town.

I was invited into the boot room after the match and, honestly, it ought to have been decked out in Mackem red and white.

The manager was the former Sunderland coach Andy King and helping us sup the beer were Denis Smith,

Malcolm Crosby and Roger Jones, who worked on the Wear but also kept goal for Newcastle of course.

Peter Reid is probably the Sunderland manager most accepted by Newcastle punters simply because he has an infectious personality and is quite capable of having a laugh at his own expense. He's known as 'monkey heed' by the majority of toonies and he goes along with it no problem.

Whenever I had to go down to Sunderland's training ground at Whitburn we used to have an impromptu football quiz, Scouse questions against Geordie ones. If it wasn't going too well Peter would call up his assistant Bobby Saxton, a one time United coach, to help him out. Cheating so and so.

Reidie was a good 'un all right and gave me a couple of Sunderland players on loan when I was at Gateshead and needed reinforcements.

XXXXX

GEORDIE Ray Kennedy was a matador of a player oozing control, power and steel.

A professional athlete of physical supremacy, Kennedy became the most decorated footballer of his generation. With first Arsenal and then Liverpool he won everything that the domestic game offered.

Yet by the age of 35 he was diagnosed with Parkinson's Disease, a progressively degenerative neurological disorder which affects the control of body movements. There is no known cure.

Parkinson's disease probably began with Ray at least 10

years before the first unequivocal physical signs and 14 years before the diagnosis was finally made.

He played excellent soccer during most of that time despite early signs of PD such as pains and cramps all along his right side, postural abnormalities affecting the right arm and leg, extreme and unexplained muscle pains in his feet, loss of normal facial and emotional expression, episodes of profound malaise, overwhelming fatigue and lack of energy. I watched in horror and despair as a good friend bravely fought a long losing battle to stay physically afloat.

Parkinson's is no respecter of ability or fame, having struck the likes of Muhammad Ali and actor Michael J Fox and today Kennedy lives in New Hartley, where his great footballing journey began, in a house adapted to his needs.

I knew Ray initially through John Maley who ran New Hartley Juniors for many, many years. Kennedy was the jewel in his crown – no matter how many players graduated into league football none have surpassed the achievements of this England international. John loved him and stayed a loyal and attentive friend through the dark days until he himself succumbed to cancer.

Another of Ray's early mates Alec Smailes, whom he got a job scouting for Liverpool and who has made a great success of it, has stayed a valued contact of mine.

At his height I ghosted Kennedy's column in the old *Football Pink* and enjoyed many a pie and a pint doing it. He was good crack our Ray.

He lived life and loved it, carousing with Jimmy Case. Batman and Robin, they were called, and Jimmy still travels up from the south coast to visit.

Often the worth of a man is revealed during adversity and while Graeme Souness may not be remembered in these parts as a manager of illuminating vision, he has been without question a great supporter of his former Liverpool team-mate away from the public eye.

Souness was a regular visitor to Ray's house when he was manager of Newcastle. Quietly and without fuss he arranged for several alterations to be made to ease his physical problems and would often take him to games at St James' Park. It was not unknown for Kennedy to sit on the Newcastle bench.

Ray was a wonderful footballer, converted from a successful Gunner centre- forward who did the double into a three-time European Cup winning left sided midfielder at Liverpool. That startling switch of position was due to the vision of a man of Durham Bob Paisley, though another top footballing man was more blind to the Kennedy charms – Sir Stanley Matthews turned him down at unglamorous Port Vale. Ray kept the letter of rejection, perhaps as a spur.

Once football had deserted his life Ray poured his energy into fundraising for the Parkinson's Disease Society, heightening awareness of the illness, until it got physically too much. He met with its most famous sufferer, Muhammad Ali, and had his picture taken with him. That photo sat in his living room.

Having topped 60 years of age Ray has almost spent as long with his terrible increasing restrictions as he did living a normal life. The man was always a fighter. He worked for the PDS until he was unable to continue. They had a 'Ray Kennedy Room' in their office.

The Lady and the Champ

YOU know you're in interesting company when a little wizened old guy in a stetson with a face as lined as a road map introduces you to his fiancée. Fiancée? Are ya sure? This guy was in his 90th year and had been married six times before while his girlfriend was a beautiful blonde lady some considerable number of years younger.

However we're talking Jake LaMotta here, a brawler fascinating enough for Hollywood legend Robert De Niro to play him in the Oscar-winning film *Raging Bull*.

Maybe the bull isn't raging quite as much these days but the show is still on the road. Denise Baker, who shares LaMotta's house in Miami with him, has muscled in on the act.

She pulls out a card and with a flourish presents it to me: 'The Lady and the Champ' it announces. Okay I get it.

I had first talked with Denise back in the States before the pair headed across the pond on a series of stop-offs promoting the old geezer. He was working in Newcastle (this was June of 2012) and I was to be his straight man. The compere, though I realised throughout the hour or so on stage that the beady eye of The Lady was fixed unerringly on me. I mustn't hassle The Champ.

Of course we're in the presence of boxing royalty and for that reason alone the whole evening on stage and in the dressing-room was fascinating. Director Martin Scorsese gave *Raging Bull* (LaMotta's 1970 autobiography) his inimitable signature and De Niro chillingly captured the menace, self loathing and corruption not only in the ring but within the murky world of the Mob which engulfed and eventually devoured boxing.

LaMotta is the last of the great old champs standing. World middleweight champion when boxing only had one version, not a host of pretenders, his brutal fists inflicted a first defeat on the iconic Sugar Ray Robinson. However the Mob lurked in the shadows every day of his life – Jake admitted taking a dive on instructions to earn himself a world title crack at Marcel Cerdan.

When we met LaMotta was fine tuned. He was a walking act. At a snap of the fingers he would come out with well rehearsed lines…

"I fought Sugar Ray so many times it's a wonder I didn't get diabetes."

"I said to Rocky Graziano one time, 'What's up there, the sun or the moon?' 'I don't know', he replied, 'I don't live round here'."

All delivered in a throaty Bronx rumble.

He got a few chuckles as much in respect of the guy as for the content or delivery.

However LaMotta's recital of the "I coulda been a contender" speech from *On the Waterfront* was quaintly touching.

Ms Baker is a former singer of the 1950s nightclub variety and an actress best known for her unclothed appearance in the 1974 production of *Let My People Come*. A musical about sexual freedom, she said.

It was she who launched *Lady and the Champ* upon unsuspecting American audiences, not always to great acclaim.

However I'm biased. I'm a boxing nut and was brought up as an impressionable kid in the LaMotta era listening on the radio to vivid word pictures painted by Raymond Glendenning of epic fights involving the likes of Joe Louis.

Therefore meeting Jake LaMotta was a bit special and to heck with the phoney goings on around him.

XXXXX

I'VE done chat shows with a load of international sporting celebs all over the North East down more years than I care to remember.

However the most unusual venue without a doubt was Durham jail. That's right, a jail with bars and naughty geezers.

These weren't characters like Norman Stanley Fletcher, Lennie Godber, Lukewarm, Harry Grout and the wimpish Officer Barraclough of H.M. Slade Prison beautifully crafted by my old mate Ian La Franais in *Porridge*.

These were seriously dangerous villains.

Brendan Foster and Steve Cram were the top athletes I was going to grill and all three of us were body searched on the way in. We did the show in the chapel which had been especially converted for the occasion. Honestly, there were more warders standing menacingly round the walls in case of an attempted mass break out (even hostage taking?) than there were prisoners sitting in orderly rows in front of us. Talk about a captive audience.

I took no comfort from the fact that if we had to take to our toes Bren and Crammie would be fine while I would probably not make it.

There were, we were told, a few lifers amongst those making up our audience and of course the guys were from all over the country so we didn't want to make it all Geordie stories. Actually we got through it all right, albeit with a few nervous laughs amongst top table guests, and at the end the prisoners lined up and filed past us to shake each of us by the hand.

The first thing we did upon emerging onto the street was seek the nearest boozer!

Crammie was a good mate for a Sunderland supporter (Bren is one of us) and I invited him to one of our Footballer of the Month awards for players from Newcastle United and Sunderland. We used a restaurant in Jesmond Dene and the lunches lasted anything up to four hours as the banter and wine flowed.

On this particular afternoon we hardly noticed as the snow came down steadily throughout the proceedings – until we ventured outside and found ourselves knee deep in the white fluffy stuff.

We had to literally dig ourselves out of the Dene only to find there was chaos on the roads with the traffic reduced to a bumper to bumper crawl. The original plan was to drop Crammie off at home and both of us were then going to get changed into evening suits complete with dicky bow ties to continue through to Durham where Steve was to receive a Sportsman of the Year award from Vaux Breweries.

However it soon became obvious that with all the chaos time was running out and we rapidly changed our plans and headed straight for Durham.

When we eventually got there a couple of hours later Crammie was still in his ordinary gear of course while the rest of the guests were resplendent in black evening suits. Oh dear, what to do.

All I decided was not lost. We found a waiter who was about the same size as Steve and headed for the toilet. The outcome was that Crammie received his award in the waiter's suit and black tie while the waiter served the meal in Steve's everyday clothes. Job done.

A Sting in the tail

THERE was a kid at St Cuthbert's Grammar School in Newcastle who was a tasty athlete.

He became the Northumberland and Durham sprint champion and at the inter-county meeting on a cinder track at Houghton he claimed that title as well. He went on to run at the national championships.

A gentle lad, he took part in the long jump and triple jump and, because of his natural pace, became a decent rugby player. His name was Gordon Sumner and he became Sting.

I seemed to know everyone who had anything to do with a young Sumner. Dave Stapylton, who used to write the schools football column for the *Chronicle*, was a classmate of said rock star in the sixties. Tony Knox who made two Amateur Cup semi-finals with Whitley Bay and played left-back for England's amateur side was Sting's PE teacher. And journo Phil Sutcliffe, who used to work with me, went on to write the official biography of The Police.

So when I was commissioned to pen a book called *Spirit*

of Tyneside, Famous Sons and Daughters, my cup certainly did runneth over on my chapter paying homage to Sting.

Contacts are so important to hacks. Sometimes it's not what you know but who you know and people like Stapylton and Knox, very much football folk to me, opened up a fascinating new insight into the school years of a superstar.

I had met Sting but would never profess to know him. These men did. Imagine a rock rebel, all blond locks and smouldering looks with a twanging guitar, and according to Stapylton you would have the completely wrong image of schoolboy Gordon.

He was described by his class mate as "a quiet, sensitive boy not a bit course. He had quite a refined voice, not a trace of a Geordie accent like some of the lads."

Cor blimey, the guy sounds like Cliff Richard.

In fact Dave and Gordon travelled to school together as 14 year olds: "I got on the train at Howden and he got on at Wallsend further down the line. We used to leave it as late as possible. I caught the train at 8.39am, he got on at Wallsend at 8.42 and the train arrived at Newcastle Central Station at 8.59am. Then it was a chase to catch the bus to the west end of the city. If we missed it we were late for school. Gordon was a sprinter so I let him set off like the wind and he held onto the bus until I got there!"

Even at that early stage Sting was a hit with the girls, long before his newly acquired blond looks on stage sent thousands of hearts fluttering. Stapylton told me of a school holiday at Loch Ailort in the Scottish Highlands near Fort William. The commandoes had used it as their training ground during the war and the kids stayed in the nissen huts which had been their barracks. It rained all week and the lads was drenched as they set off home.

"We caught the train to Mallaig, a fishing port, and spent half an hour there before moving on to Fort William. While we were in Mallaig two girls latched on to Gordon. He wore a PVC raincoat, which were all the rage at the time, and looked dead modern. They came with us on the train to Fort William where we all went to see *The Great St Trinians Train Robbery* at the pictures.

"Both girls sat with Gordon. He was a bit embarrassed but dead chuffed that he had scored. The rest of us were envious. There were only two girls and Gordon had them both. I've often wondered since if they realise the young lad in the raincoat was Sting."

Tony Knox remembered Sumner the sprinter: "He was a natural, someone with unbelievable ability. All the top sprinters have the knack of looking relaxed when they perform and so had Gordon. I was always onto him.

'You're not trying lad,' I would say. He had a clipped style of running and looked to be putting in no effort."

My book *The Spirit of Tyneside* showcased the best of our talent. Apart from Sting I did chapters on the likes of Ian La Frenais, Rowan Atkinson, Catherine Cookson, Cardinal Basil Hume, Sir John Hall and Bobby and Jack Charlton. It's the only one of my 16 books written previous to this one which wasn't purely sport. I enjoyed the change. Interviewing Catherine Cookson and Rowan Atkinson was a tad different to Gazza and George Best!

xxxxx

BROTHERS they may be and, sure, there is a definite facial likeness but Jack and Bobby Charlton are very different men.

Yes we know that in later life they sadly haven't been as close as families ought to be. It's been an open secret. However even in the days of blood brothers in arms they approached life from a very different perspective.

Jack was a bit of a scally while Bobby was, according his mam Cissie, "just like Little Lord Fauntleroy."

I loved Cissie. Snowy haired and in her seventies, she was a warm, cuddly lady who embraced life. She described Jack as being much more like her, outspoken and to the point. "Jack was the mixer, full of life and go like me. Bobby was shy to the point of appearing big headed."

Jack put it rather more bluntly when we were reminiscing over a jar of the good stuff: "Bobby was a pain in the backside to me as a kid. He's two and a half years younger than me and was a mother's boy. I had to take him with me wherever I went. I wanted to be off bird nesting and blackberrying but my mother would say, 'Take our Bobby and look after him.' I didn't like that.

"I used to say, 'I'm not tekkin' wor kid, he's ower soft.' But I still had to."

Chuck a football into the equation of course and Bobby was the swan, a gifted footballer of grace, style and balance, whereas Jack was the ugly duckling – all knobbly knees, ungainly gait, and aggression. Both, however, were World Cup winners and as such the most famous brothers of English soccer.

Carrying David

HOLLYWOOD ought to make a film based round Glenn McCrory becoming the North East's first ever world champion when he ripped the IBF cruiser crown off the head of a cocky Patrick Lumumba.

Not just because McCrory did it when working on the pads with his missus in their living room and signing on at the local dole office. And I don't champion his cause because he's my best mate, a guy who has gone round the globe with me enough times to have our heads spinning. No, it's the incredible story behind that epic night of June 3, 1989 that makes for a celluloid tear jerker which would even top Sylvester Stallone's fictional *Rocky*.

There's a huge poster on one of the walls of Glenn's apartment in Jesmond emblazoned with the words: 'Carrying David.' Above is a silhouette of an older boy with a youngster on his back. It's Glenn and his brother.

A film script, tinkered with over and over again, has been in the hands of film makers for around 10 years now. We –

Glenn and I and others – actually sat with one producer, a young lady, on the lawns of our rented villa in the south of France during the Cannes Film Festival discussing the finer points of a deal. Hence the poster.

Hollywood and their like take an awful long time mulling over most projects it would seem. Ask Stallone – his *Rocky* also met with a lot of promises but little concrete action until his major breakthrough.

So what is McCrory's tale? It's a remarkable and true story of the unique bond that develops between two brothers, one destined to become a world champion, the other disabled, wheelchair bound, and terminally ill. Together the two boys confront the odds, inspiring each other to overcome their fears and realise extraordinary ambitions. *Rocky* meets *My Left Foot* is how Glenn describes it.

McCrory triumphed at the Louisa Leisure Centre in Stanley little more than a mile away from the house in which he was born and only 200 yards away from his home at the time. That's remarkable in itself, while the headline on an article in *The Sun* that very morning written by a mate of both of us Colin Hart declared 'Glenn's a Goner.' That's how much Lumumba was rated.

However the sweetest moment of all came as an elated and victorious McCrory scanned the smiling, cheering faces of so many folk he knew personally. There in his wheelchair sat David, proud as a peacock, his eyes shining. Tears welled in big brother's eyes. He didn't even know David was present.

Police had knocked on the McCrory door and said: "Come on, David should be there." He was lifted into a squad car and shot round to the local venue of hope and dreams. It was a thoughtful and totally unexpected act by the boys in blue, a wonderful moment as Glenn's arm was raised in gladiatorial triumph.

David had been fostered by the McCrorys when he was seven years old, a boy who always had a smile on his face. He was small, unlike the strapping young McCrory boys, and walked with a slight limp.

There were already six kids in the house, aged between two and 12, but David was loved as one of the family. He didn't walk too well and Glenn used to carry him to school on his back. Little did we know David was terminally ill.

Slowly David got worse and when he was 15 the doctors told the family what the problem was, muscular dystrophy, and that he would inevitably die. A year later he was gone.

Now you know why victory over Lumumba mattered so much. It was the moment two brothers tasted the joys of life as one. It was, too, a stonking victory because it wasn't expected by those who considered themselves sound judges of boxing flesh.

I remember having a pint with pop star PJ Proby – he of the split trousers – at the leisure centre bar before being allowed into Glenn's dressing-room just prior to his entry into the ring. Hacks didn't get in there. Not before a fight anyway. However we shared a bond of our own.

We didn't say much. I watched as Glenn paced up and down banging his gloves together, a dressing-gown covering his pale torso. He was in his own zone. When he caught my eye we hugged. That said more than words.

It was thought McCrory would start cautiously feeling out his opponent, waiting to see what he had to offer. Instead

Glenn almost ran to the centre of the ring and, territory claimed, he set about pummelling his opponent. It startled Lumumba and set the tone of the fight. The crowd were alight. The noise deafening. McCrory had grabbed the initiative and never let go.

xxxxx

I'VE always got on quite well with referees, the policemen of football. It's the masochist in them that intrigues me. I ghosted the autobiography of Pat Partridge and Alan Wilkie sent me a personally signed copy of his book *One Night At The Palace*.

I examined the inside of a few nightclubs and hostelries with Ken Redfern, visited the County Durham home of George Courtney on more than one occasion, and have spent pleasant time in the company of the North East's latest two superstar whistlers Mark Clattenburg and Michael Oliver. All good lads.

Of course referees are only human (despite what you might think matey) and like all of us support their hometown teams, which is why their bosses tend to steer them well clear of matches involving their own.

However it's logically impossible to avoid all conflicts of interest, which is why Alan Wilkie found himself in something of an uneasy situation on the last day of the 1991-92 season.

Alan is a lifelong Newcastle United fan and, you may recall, Kevin Keegan had just taken over with the Mags staring at relegation to the Third Division for the first time in their history if all didn't go well that fateful day. Newcastle were at Leicester but if Oxford United won at Tranmere then all would be lost anyway, it was believed. The trouble was Wilkie was the ref at Prenton Park.

Oxford supporters were in party mood as is often the case on the last day and they arrived dressed as Egyptians, Pharaohs and Mummies. The carnival atmosphere must have been caught by the Oxford players because they won 2-1. Alan was in utter dismay. His beloved Newcastle were guillotined.

He was slumped in the referee's room, his face like a yard of tripe, when the door opened and in walked Oxford manager Brian Horton. Why, he enquired, did Alan look so dejected "when you've had a good game?"

Wilkie told his sorry tale but a baffled Horton explained that Newcastle had actually won at Leicester through a late own goal. Wilkie still looked like a well smacked bum.

'It doesn't make any difference,' he said miserably. Manager and referee were now poring over the league table and working out facts and figures. Suddenly a lifeline. Lo and behold Plymouth Argyle had come into the frame and because they had lost it was they who went down. Wilkie was now a dog with two tails.

Of course it was the turning point for the Mags. They stormed to promotion the following season and, as Keegan built the Entertainers, became Premier League runners up.

Wilkie became infamous as the referee who sent off Eric Cantona at Crystal Palace, turning him into Bruce Lee as he karate kicked a mickey-taking fan on his way off the field. Hence the title of his book *One Night At The Palace*.

Life is eventful when you're a whistler AND a Newcastle fan.

Why Smokin' Joe hated Ali

SOME bitter rivalries mellow with the passing of years and conversations are resumed where once the only contact would be a spit in the eye.

However with Joe Frazier he never forgave Muhammad Ali for what he perceived as grave slights upon himself. Even though Ali has been reduced to a shell through the crippling effects of Parkinson's disease, Smokin' Joe's ice cold heart never melted. He took his bitter dislike to the grave.

I spent some considerable time with Frazier in Newcastle and an amiable man with great recall was charm itself – until Ali was mentioned. Then the vitriol came spewing out. It was shuddering in its ferocity yet it must be admitted that what Ali had said about him in their prime also went well beyond the restraints of decency. Black man insulted black man with open racial abuse.

By now – shortly before his death – Frazier was suffering himself. He had diabetes and high blood pressure. He walked with the help of a steel cane after a car accident.

Yet he openly attacked and scoffed at Ali's physical deterioration, insisting it was the Lord's way of punishing and silencing his egotistical spiel. As for Ali's sad appearance when lighting the Olympic flame of 1996, Frazier expressed grief that he couldn't be there to shove Ali into the fires. He repeated it to me years later. It became apparent the more we talked that while Ali's baiting during their three epic fights had much to do with a poisonous hatred, it went deeper than that.

Frazier had helped out Ali with friendship and money when he was at his lowest during the Vietnam years, viewed not as The Greatest but a draft dodger and a country turned its back on him. Yet all Joe got in return was publicly ridiculed. Ali taunted Frazier for being an Uncle Tom. In response Smokin' Joe repeatedly insulted Ali by calling him by his birth name Clay.

As the 1970s laboured on Ali's taunts toward Frazier became less political and more indefensible. When their epic 1975 fight in Manila loomed Ali repeatedly called Frazier "a gorilla." He spoke verses on how "black and ugly" Frazier was. For Ali, it was part of the show. For Frazier it was more scarring than any punch in Ali's arsenal. "I whupped that guy three times," he growled at me, "but they only gave me the verdict once."

The way Joe Frazier justified his stance to me was that he was the 1964 Olympic gold medallist. He never dodged a draft. He never boasted of throwing his medal in the Ohio River. He never said "God damn America." Yet there was Ali lighting the Olympic torch while he was sitting at home. The establishment had chosen the anti-hero, and Joe Frazier was cast merely as the foil and the fool.

It was one of the most startling and unrelenting displays of hatred festering inside a man and made me greatly uncomfortable. Ali has always been a hero of mine for his shuddering ability and quick wit, his bravery and at times childlike twinkle, while Frazier was a proud warrior, not a stylist boxer, who was indeed something special himself and under different circumstances when his taunter was forgotten, a man of simple charm.

While their epic fights stand alone above most things, I prefer to think of Muhammad Ali and Joe Frazier as men apart because in that way I can appreciate both. Perhaps I don't understand because I have never faced such personal hostility. If that is so then I am eternally grateful.

XXXXX

WHEN I was a schoolboy with nothing but a pocketful of dreams I used to frequent the County Ground in Jesmond where I marvelled at the flannelled heroes of Northumberland. One of them was KD Smith, a tall bespectacled all-rounder who had tasted the heights of first class cricket. Years later I got to know one of his sons Paul Smith, common by name but most certainly not by nature.

Paul was one of the first rock 'n' roll cricketers. Good looking with a mop of long blond hair and a devilish grin, Paul threw away a perfectly good career with a trophy winning Warwickshire through the joys of temptation. Birds, booze and, aye, the curse of his age. Drugs.

It copped him a 10-year ban from the game which affectively finished his career and saw him put down the bat to take up the pen. He wrote his own autobiography – it showed round the rough edges – and cheekily called it *Wasted?* You know, a wasted talent and wasted on drugs.

A scoundrel, maybe, irresponsible unquestionably, but he was infectious was our Paul. He came to see me during a self-styled publicity tour for his penned life story and stayed recounting wilder and wilder yarns way beyond our allotted time. We kept in constant touch after that.

Amongst his ditties tossed around like confetti was a team-mate's claim that he lost his virginity with a chicken and the story of the Sinn Fein leaders Gerry Adams and Martin McGuinness being asked to play a game of cricket against John Major's government.

There was also the time, inevitably, he joined the mile-high club on a pre-season flight to Cape Town. When the toilet door was forced open and a sheepish Smith returned to his seat, Warwickshire coach Bob Woolmer angrily asked: "Were you wearing your club blazer when the doors were opened?" Smith chortled: "I laughed at the absurdity of the whole situation. I believe that was the moment he washed his hands of me and that I'd become a lost cause."

He recalled with more clarity than he could muster on the day going out to bat at Bournemouth against Malcolm Marshall of all people when "three sheets to the wind".

"Don't worry, Smitty boy,' Malcolm said, "this won't take long." He was as good as his word. After a few minutes Smith was on my way – initially walking in the wrong direction away from the pavilion!

It was Oscar Wilde who said he could resist anything but temptation. However it was Paul Smith who confirmed it.

I'm all right Jack

HE WAS as mad as a box of frogs. With his big bulging eyes and mischievous glint he was the ultimate practical joker.

Whenever Newcastle United were on their travels Jack Fairbrother would pull up his overcoat collar, get his goalkeeper's flat cap out, and go begging round startled commuters on the railway platform. Life was a breeze.

Yet as a keeper Fairbrother was a perfectionist who left nothing to chance. He had more angles than a London spiv. In training he would tie a rope to a goalpost and give the other end to Jackie Milburn or one of the other forwards. As the striker ran in to shoot the rope would indicate exactly where Jack should be standing to take the shot. Consequently he rarely had to throw himself around during a match, as the ball inevitably came to his chest.

A copper during the war, Fairbrother used to go down to Market Street Police Station and get a pair of their white gloves used for directing traffic. They were his stock in trade on matchdays. Mad Jack only played in one of the three fifties FA Cup finals, the first one of 1951. United's best team of the three according to Wor Jackie.

The sadness was that as the champagne flowed back at Newcastle's hotel, tongues became looser and looser and Fairbrother overheard a director saying: "It's the last game he plays for us – he's finished now."

Crush and humiliated Jack slipped away from the party, bags packed, to go home. Luckily Joe Harvey and Bobby Mitchell gave chase and hauled him back to the celebrations from the platform of King's Cross station.

As it happened it was nearly all over. Fairbrother broke his collarbone against Manchester United in the September of the following season and never played football again. It was particularly sad because Jack didn't make his Football League debut until he was approaching 30 year of age. The Second World War had confined him to non-competitive wartime appearances.

I got to know Jack well after his glory days. First when he was fleetingly manager of Gateshead and later when as Gateshead chairman we played at Kettering where ex-Newcastle director Peter Mallinger was the boardroom supremo. Peter always invited old Newcastle players to sit in the director's box and Fairbrother lived nearby at Titchmarsh.

He would, all pop eyed, recall the stories I've just told in great detail over a half-time cuppa.

Would he have become a good manager like his old '51 team-mate Joe Harvey?

I don't know because tragedy struck to effectively end that

career too. He was a rookie boss at Coventry City as United approached the third of their three Wembley finals but his wife fell down stairs at home and was killed, leaving him a widower with two young children.

Fairbrother's successor in the '52 and '55 finals was Ronnie Simpson, a very different keeper. Where Mad Jack was all about angles and shots coming to chest, Ronnie was spidery legged and through lack of inches was a reflex liner rather than a man who dominated his penalty box plucking balls out of the air. Simpson walked on the balls of his feet ready to spring and saved as many shots with his legs as hands.

He was to go on and have a fabulous second career back in his native Scotland, keeping goal for Celtic in a winning European Cup final at the age of 36 and seven months – a whole 15 years after his Cup final with Newcastle. This a guy who was the youngest player ever to appear in the Scottish first class game at 14 years and 304 days for Queen's Park and the oldest international debutant at 36 years and 196 days. Honestly Methuselah didn't last as long!

The last time I saw Ronnie was in early February of 2004 when he travelled down from Scotland for the funeral of his Cup final team-mate Bob Stokoe at the Newcastle Crematorium. We had a good old natter for quite a while, obviously recalling the fab fifties. Ronnie looked great and appeared fit as a lop. Two months later he died suddenly of a heart attack.

XXXXX

IT'S not often a hack takes over as owner of a football

club. How many can you name? Anyway part of the job of a chairman is to deal with very delicate matters, which if they became public knowledge at a certain time during negotiations could jeopardise the whole kit and kaboodle.

At the conclusion of that day's talks during some such dealings, the rest of the board were rising and heading for the door.

"Gentlemen," I boomed. "Whatever you do don't tell the Press!"

Back came one sharp reply: "But can we talk it over with you chairman?"

When life
wasn't Fab

**IF YOU lived in the hellhole of the Bronx, where
life was cheap and gangs settled scores with a gun,
would you dare call your son Fabulous? Surely that's
a total contradiction of life and is asking for trouble.
Like Johnny Cash and a boy named Sue.**

However to Luce the Juice her kids were her ray of light
in a grim and dangerous world so Fabulous Flournoy it
was and, just for good measure, she called two of his sisters
Divine and Precious. One ballsy mother! Luce the Juice, I
should explain, was the nickname for Fab's mam and he
is of course the record-breaking coach of the Newcastle
Eagles basketball team that has rewritten the record books.

Down the years I've spent many an hour in countless
coffee shops with Fab recalling our lives and hopes, the
knocks and the joys, the relentless pursuit of perfection in
sport, he with the Eagles, me with Gateshead. He was as
interested in my philosophy at the International Stadium as
I was his. Once he offered me a seat on the Eagles bench

on play night to watch him work at close range. I somehow doubt if Alan Pardew would be willing to give such insight at Newcastle United.

Fab turned up at my surprise birthday party a couple of years or so ago. He gives willingly of his time. The tales he told me about the Bronx were of abject poverty and danger where people hustled, ran drugs, stole and carried guns just to stay alive. Not that everyone did of course. Fab's older brother, who looked after him, was slain in a nightclub at the age of 22 and his little brother took a bullet in the chest walking to the local store. He survived but only just.

Even after escaping to England through basketball, heartache was only a phone call away. Like the call to his Newcastle apartment not that long ago. Two of his friends had been driving home, he was told, when they pulled up by the side of the pavement and an egg was thrown at the car. Fab's closest mate who was driving got out, angry at the mess, and ran over to ask why the lad had done it. As he approached the kid pulled out a gun and shot him in the head. He died instantly.

Such are the dangers of life that Fab's mother became a 'transporter' in the murky world of drugs to try and earn a crust for her poverty-stricken family. What else could a girl on her own do when, having moved to New York City from the Deep South, she had her first child at 15 years of age and a second − Fab − at 17. Without a father in sight, without being able to read or write. Without education, hope or help.

"She had no education so she sold drugs, transported them, just to survive," explained Flournoy. "We never stayed in one place long, we moved from abandoned building to abandoned building. Shelters to shelters. We couldn't even qualify for welfare – what you call the dole in this country. Suddenly she started making money fast and when my younger brother and sister came along we were rich compared to the way we had been!

"But it was no life, no way to live. And inevitably something went wrong with one of the transports. We were all in danger – I remember coming home from school to find mam with all the bags packed. Within 20 minutes we'd gone. I didn't go back to school for three months. It was the roughest of times."

However mam eventually educated herself as best she could and remains today the inspiration for a loving and grateful Fab. She has with his help left the mean streets of the Bronx for a safer place. Life is getting better but the old days will never be forgotten by mother or son.

xxxxx

DAVA was a hard little so-and-so. Small man, big heart certainly summed him up. John Davison was a Geordie who early days liked to see himself as a wheeler dealer. You know, a bit like Del Boy. This time next year I'll be a millionaire.

I first got to know him as a more than decent amateur boxer around Newcastle but when he didn't get the nod to go to the 1988 Olympic Games he chucked it in disgust. 'End of', we all thought. After all John was pushing the wrong end of his twenties.

However a local gangster Viv Graham, who had been an amateur fighter himself, kept pushing Davison to turn pro. Graham effectively ran large slices of Newcastle. He was an underworld godfather who was gunned down leaving a local boozer on New Year's Eve of 1993.

Like a lot of hard men from the streets he loved boxing and football. In his case Newcastle United. Graham bankrolled Dava, who never shied off promoting his backer, and Sunderland manager Tommy Conroy signed him up. Game on. Dava couldn't afford to waste time at his age and he roared through the pro ranks, a real crowd pleaser willing to take a punch to land one. Every John Davison fight was a tear up, a war. He became British champion and the WBC International featherweight belt winner in only his 11th paid bout.

His breakthrough fight was at Hartlepool's Borough Hall, a real boxing venue, with Thai champion Srikoon Narachawat his opponent. Inevitably Dava sparked him. Now folk were taking notice and a local businessman Jimmy Stanley paid for John and his family to have a two-week holiday in Tenerife. "It was the first time I'd gone abroad without having to take my boxing gloves," Davison told me.

Inevitably being a chancer John entered a Best Dressed Woman competition organised for geezers at his hotel. He put on his wife Carol's knee length skirt and crop top, a thong, and a pair of her shoes. His face was done up a treat. And of course he won – despite his skinhead. It was his second title win in a month!

Dava may have been fun, and still is, but the fight game was a serious business to him. Tommy Conroy would often wax lyrical about John knocking on his door on Christmas Day begging Tommy to open up the gym so he could work out. With Glenn McCrory and Billy Hardy as well as Dava this was a golden period for North East boxing.

The Impossible
Dream

IAN PORTERFIELD was a man whose life was punctuated by drama. He scored Sunderland's goal that caused one of the biggest FA Cup final upsets of all time in 1973, only for a car crash the following year to leave him fighting for his life with a fractured skull and broken jaw. Survive he did but by the relatively young age of 61, when coach of Armenia, he died of colon cancer in a Surrey hospice.

Though a Newcastle man I was at Wembley to see Porter of the Second Division destroy the might of Leeds United. I had got to know him through talk-ins I did across the North East and he actually asked me to write his book. We called it *The Impossible Dream*. A no-brainer really.

As we talked deep into many a night it became obvious how as underdogs Sunderland relaxed in the build-up to their big day. Don Revie had dared to state openly in Wembley week that the Mackems had dropped a clanger taking the players away for a week. Boredom, he declared, would only add to the tension before D day. Boredom? I think not. On the Wednesday of final week Porterfield, Dennis Tueart and Billy Hughes were at a recording of *Top Of The Pops* mixing with the likes of the Sweet, Hot Chocolate and Suzy Quatro.

The next evening the whole team was at the Football Writers' dinner enjoying a meal and a bit of banter. Revie banned Leeds players of course. Even on the Friday, match eve, the same Three Musketeers from *Top Of The Pops* recorded a radio show for DJ Emperor Rosko.

Mind you, Ian still carried a barrowload of superstitions into the Wembley dressing-room. He wasn't leaving that to chance. Chortling at the stupidity of it all he ran me through the list: a lucky horseshoe from the babysitter's mother (a proper shoe and not one of those fancy silver ones); a rabbit's foot given by a young girl when he was playing for Raith Rovers; a Kennedy coin which belonged to his grandad; and a Cowdenbeath and District schools' football medal which belonged to his uncle Ian who was killed in the pits when he was only 19. Blimey, he would need more than a haversack to transport that lot!

At least one of them must have worked of course. Porterfield was one of only three outfield players not to have scored a Cup goal – Dick Malone and Richie Pitt were the others – and then he strikes the most precious ever.

After Ian died in September of 2007 his family got in touch with me to ask how they might be able to get a copy of our book. It was out of publication of course and I had only a single book myself. I was sad I couldn't help.

Then lo and behold a few weeks later while I was browsing amongst the second hand books at the market on

Tynemouth Station there it was. *The Impossible Dream* with a photo of Ian with the FA Cup perched proudly on his head. Happy memories.

xxxxx

IT'S NOT often you worry for someone's life. I did exactly that when Glenn McCrory was roasted like a pig on a spit to make the cruiserweight limit and sacrificed his world title to the brutal hands of Jeff Lampkin.

The other time was when Billy Hardy travelled over to Laredo in Texas for his return world IBF bantamweight title fight with one of the weight's all time greats Orlando Canizales. Billy is a carrot-topped little fella with pale, pale skin and there he was thrust into a boxing ring in some car park under the blazing midday Texan sun and told to perform against the local hero's thirst for glory. Good gracious, I was issued with a fan as well as a Press pass when I entered the tinderbox and, boy, did I need it.

The high noon showdown was so that the fight could be beamed back live to England but couldn't it have been in some nice air conditioned arena? Not on your nelly, not after the shock Billy had handed the world champion back in Sunderland when he took him the distance and almost nicked the decision on a split vote.

No, Hardy had to get out there in 123 degree heat and you boil a chicken at 120 degrees. His red hair and fair skin acted like a magnet to the great orange ball in the sky.

However strength can be sapped but not a big heart and Billy possessed plenty of that. He was hit so hard in the third round that he literally somersaulted almost on top of me ringside. I thought he was coming to sit on my knee and share my cooling fan. The sweat was oozing out of him. Yet Hardy kept going until the eighth before, looking like a rag doll, Canizales finally brought the torture to an end.

Laredo was quite a place. I travelled in the company of only one other reporter Graham Robinson, an amazing man. He had a false arm from birth but was a terrific league cricketer smashing the ball with willow despite a one handed grip and bowling like a good 'un.

Our hotel was on the banks of the Rio Grande river and we used to watch the Mexicans every morning trying to swim across to a better life and disappear into the bricks of Laredo. A risky business with border control officers prowling the north river bank.

We spent some time in the company of Billy's trainer Richard Smith, a handsome South African with a passion and belief in the wee man. Imagine my utter shock and disbelief when Hardy told me some time later that Richard had died in a hail of bullets back home.

Evidently Richard was killed in front of his two kids by car thieves he had disturbed at his house.

Hardy was ready to quit after Laredo (May 1991) but he didn't and such was his undeniable pedigree that he went on to have more great success. Every fighter will tell you if you box abroad with a title on the line you have to knock the guy out to get a draw.

That makes you realise the class of Billy to win the European feather title against Mehdi Labdouni in France, successfully defend it against Stefano Zoff in Italy, and then come home to defeat Steve Robinson, a long time world champion who defeated our own John Davison.

Billy drops into my local pub from time to time and it's always good to see him.

In loving memory

IN SEPTEMBER of 2009 I attended Durham Cathedral for a memorial service to Sir Bobby Robson. I had been close like so many. The day touched me deeply. I would like to finish by reproducing the article I filed here in full. It was written from the heart:

THE PRIVILEGED walked through a heavy oak door into 900 years of history. Durham Cathedral, a majestic Norman monument since 1093 nestling on a peninsula created by a large loop in the River Wear, flung open its arms to pay homage to a miner's son from down the road.

Bobby Robson was of our stock, a common man who became very uncommon in his chosen world of professional football. So much so that, not only was he made a knight of the realm kneeling ram rod of back before the Prince of Wales and was now honoured in the shrine of the north east's best loved saint Cuthbert, but is so adored by the public. He united soccer tribes and won the hearts of young as well as old.

Sir Bobby's standing is such that the world halted to pay its respects and the 75-minute service was beamed back live to three football grounds where once he ruled – St James' Park a few miles away, Portman Road in rural East Anglia, and Craven Cottage in the heart of the capital. Yesterday Durham also became a cathedral of football.

They arrived in their droves from wide and far, the great and the good 1,000 in total. Paul Mariner, his old centre-forward of Ipswich and England, had flown in from America, former England boss Steve McClaren arrived late from Holland as did Bobby's old captain at PSV Eindhoven, Barcelona president Joan Laporta and manager Pep Guardiola headed a 10-man deputation from Catalonia.

If this mighty building, which took 40 years to complete, has witnessed much down the vast passage of time, rarely if ever can football's royalty have passed through its doors in such vast numbers.

While Sir Alex Ferguson and Gary Lineker held centre stage, giving moving and often witty tributes to the Great Man, the pews were heaving to the collective weight of the likes of Alan Shearer, David Seaman, Paul Gascoigne, Fabio Capello, Sven-Goran Eriksson, Bobby Charlton, Lawrie McMenemy, Peter Reid, Shay Given, Jermaine Jenas, David Moyes, Sir Trevor Brooking, Graham Taylor, Bryan Robson, Peter Beardsley, Malcolm Macdonald, Terry McDermott, Terry Butcher, Steve Bruce, Stuart Pearce, Kevin Beattie, Bob Moncur, Sam Allardyce, Eric Gates and literally a bus load of Newcastle United players.

Roy Keane avoided the television cameras outside sneaking round the edge of the media pack, Jack Charlton did likewise wearing his trademark cloth cap and shooting jacket, while United super fans Ant and Dec walked the walk.

Lady Elsie, tiny but wearing a large brimmed black hat and flanked by her sons Paul, Andrew and Mark who so resemble their father, was ushered past us all to seats of natural privilege.

"Praise my soul the king of heaven" reverberated round the great hall as suddenly the place lit with the mass warmth of those who loved a public figure described by the Very Reverend Michael Sadgrove, the Dean of Durham, as "a national treasure and marvellous man." Between stirring hymns including soccer's own *Abide With Me*, sung by every footballer and fan who ever set foot inside Wembley on FA Cup final afternoon including Bobby of course, the tributes flowed beginning with Tom Wilson who in 1950 joined Fulham on the same day as Robson and was to become best man at his wedding.

Tom shared digs with Bobby for five years until his marriage to Elsie, a North East nurse, at the young age of 22. He recalled their love of spam fritters, purchased on a weekly wage of £7, and of their plans to go together on an Ashes tour of Australia. A lifetime's ambition thwarted at the end when cancer returned for the fifth time to weaken and finally claim Sir Bobby. "We will never see his like again," finished Tom Wilson and there wasn't a dry eye in the place.

Gary Lineker was next up, striding into the pulpit from which a photo of Bobby hung proudly. The Bobby we loved and will remember with thick white thatch, jaw jutting, twinkle in the eye, smile flickering upon his lips. Lineker spoke of his "extreme good fortune" to reach his peak when Bobby Robson was England manager – "a brilliant leader of men and singularly the most enthusiastic and passionate man I ever met in football." You could almost see heads nodding row by row. Churchillian is how Lineker described Bobby's team talks while bravery as well as sound judgement personified his managerial style – gambling on two tiny forwards, Lineker and Peter Beardsley, switching to a three-man last line of defence at Italia '90 which swept England to the World Cup semi-finals, and winning the dressing room by being "hugely supportive and fiercely loyal" to his players.

Fergie followed immediately, his Glaswegian accent cutting through the BBC vowels of Lineker.

"Bobby always knew his roots," maintained the Manchester United boss. "It was fantastic that he never changed, he was always the man from the mining community of his beloved North East. It was a great talent that."

Ferguson, too, talked of bravery which Bobby personified to the very end in his fight against the ravages of cancer.

"He took a decision very few English managers ever do – to manage abroad. Not in one but three countries and very successfully too before coming back to his beloved Newcastle United." It was left to Prof Ruth Plummer, a non footballing person, to carry Bobby's story to its conclusion with his startling drive to raise money through his Sir Bobby Robson Foundation so that all future cancer sufferers can receive even more help.

"He took on this battle like all the others," declared Prof Plummer. "I came to know a warm and generous man who always had time to chat and ask other patients how they were feeling." As I listened I couldn't help but recall when I flew over to Portugal to spend a few precious days with him. We sat on the rocks overlooking the Atlantic and he recalled, without a flicker of self pity, how cancer had first struck him down. He won that fight and three more but finally was beaten though displaying supreme dignity to the very end.

We met in his last few months as well, when he held one arm in support and had a pronounced limp. Yet again the talk was of Newcastle United and his desire to raise money for the cause. Passion still flowed from every pore. While the service was peppered with spoken tributes to United's last successful manager there were other moments to warm the hearts of the converted.

Welsh soprano Katherine Jenkins, who met Sir Bobby 18 months ago and became a close friend, lent a cooling, soaring voice to the occasion. "Holy Jesu, who takes away the sins of the world, grant them rest."

When Tenors Unlimited sang *Nessun Dorma* I swear the great stained windows of a mighty cathedral almost cracked. We were all back at Italia '90...Gazza's tears, Lineker's finger to one eye imploring Bobby to watch him, Chris Waddle's soaring penalty which flew so high the moon ducked. We could see each and every moment so vividly once again.

Just when we thought the tributes of the soccer mad had given way to more formal Christian talk the Right Reverend Martin Wharton, Bishop of Newcastle, informed us that he is, in fact, a Magpie fan and season ticket holder at St James'

Park which lent extra poignancy to his description of Bobby as "a footballing colossus" whose life was always black and white. As a young lad, a trainee electrician at the local pit with hobnailed boots and tin hat the tools of his trade, adult life started in darkness deep beneath the soil of his native Durham. Early memories were of him and his dad washing away coal dust turning from black to white as they did so every single night.

"Bobby was to enjoy another black and white experience with his dad on the terraces of his great love St James's," said the Bishop of Newcastle. "He lived, breathed and slept football." Maybe we had lost Bobby, aged 76, but this was a joyous occasion to celebrate his life. If the skies shed rain by the bucket loads outside we smiled and laughed openly at the warm heartedness of Bobby's existence. To witness his crumpled face wreathed in smiles was to experience joy.

As we were waiting to leave Gazza passed by, giving me a wink and a thumbs up. The tears of 1990 and upon Bobby's death back in July long gone, a tortured spirit uplifted by warm memories. Outside as the bells peeled and we all talked to old friends of our special memories of Sir Robert I spotted three choirboys, still in their purple cassocks, sprinting down the lawns to get their hymn sheets signed by the many famous footballers who today were just bit part players.

Somehow I think Sir Bobby Robson would have liked that!